Duden

WISSEN » ÜBEN » TESTEN

Englisch

3., aktualisierte Auflage

6. Klasse

Dudenverlag
Berlin • Mannheim • Zürich

Bibliografische Information der Deutschen Nationalbibliothek
Die Deutsche Nationalbibliothek verzeichnet diese Publikation in der
Deutschen Nationalbibliografie; detaillierte bibliografische
Daten sind im Internet über http://dnb.d-nb.de abrufbar.

Das Wort **Duden** ist für den Verlag Bibliographisches Institut GmbH
als Marke geschützt.

Alle Rechte vorbehalten.
Nachdruck, auch auszugsweise, vorbehaltlich der Rechte,
die sich aus den Schranken des UrhG ergeben, nicht gestattet.

© Duden 2013   D C B
Bibliographisches Institut GmbH
Mecklenburgische Straße 53, 14197 Berlin

Redaktionelle Leitung Anika Donner
Redaktion Martin Fruhstorfer, Dr. Anja Steinhauer
Autorinnen Birgit Hock, Petra Nagel, Annette Schomber, Linda Strehl,
Dr. Anja Steinhauer (Klappe)
Sprecher Alison Ripier, Michael Shiels

Herstellung Andreas Preising
Layout Horst Bachmann
Illustration Carmen Strzelecki
Umschlaggestaltung Glas AG, Seeheim-Jugenheim
Umschlagabbildung shutterstock.com / Dmitriy Shironosov

Satz Katrin Kleinschrot, Stuttgart
Druck und Bindung Heenemann GmbH & Co. KG
Bessemerstraße 83–91, 12103 Berlin
Printed in Germany

ISBN 978-3-411-72143-6

Inhaltsverzeichnis

1 Adjektive und Adverbien

1.1 Adjektive 5
1.2 Adverbien der Art und Weise 9
1.3 Adjektive und Adverbien im Vergleich 13

Klassenarbeit 1–2 16

2 Modale Hilfsverben

2.1 Das Hilfsverb *können* 21
2.2 Das Hilfsverb *dürfen* 23
2.3 Das Hilfsverb *müssen* 25

Klassenarbeit 1–2 30

3 Vergangenheit

3.1 Das *simple past* 34
3.2 Das *simple past* bei unregelmäßigen Verben 37
3.3 Das *past progressive* 41
3.4 Das *present perfect* 44
3.5 Zeitformen der Vergangenheit im Vergleich 51
   Wichtige unregelmäßige Verben 52

Klassenarbeit 1–3 56

4 Zukunft

4.1 Das *will-future* 63
4.2 Das *going to-future* 66
4.3 *Will-future* und *going to-future* im Vergleich 69

Klassenarbeit 1–2 72

5 Der Satz

5.1 Bejahte Aussagesätze 76
5.2 Verneinte Aussagesätze 79
5.3 Bedingungssätze 83
5.4 Relativsätze 86

Klassenarbeit 1–3 93

6 Fragen

6.1 *Simple past* und *past progressive* 99
6.2 *Present perfect* 106

Klassenarbeit 1–2 108

7 Englisch lernen

7.1 Mit dem Wörterbuch umgehen 112
7.2 Hörverstehen 116
7.3 Englisch sprechen 120
7.4 Besser lesen und verstehen 122

Klassenarbeit 1 125

Stichwortfinder 128

Adjektive und Adverbien

1.1 Adjektive

Adjektive *(adjectives)* beschreiben Lebewesen, Dinge oder Ereignisse näher. Mit ihnen kannst du angeben, *wie* jemand oder etwas ist.

Größe: big, tall (Menschen), small
Farbe: blue, brown, red, green
Eigenschaft: crazy, intelligent, stupid, nice

Die Steigerung von Adjektiven

Mithilfe von Adjektiven kann man Menschen und Dinge vergleichen. Dazu benötigt man Steigerungsformen: den Komparativ (Vergleichsstufe) und den Superlativ (Höchststufe). Man steigert:
Positiv (Grundstufe) → Komparativ → Superlativ.

Andy is tall. Steven is taller. But Rick is the tallest boy.

Es gibt zwei Formen der Steigerung:
Die Steigerung mit **-er** und **-est** gilt für
- einsilbige Adjektive,
- zweisilbige Adjektive, die auf *-y* enden.

cheap → cheaper → cheapest
happy → happier → happiest

Mit **more** und **most** werden gesteigert:
- zwei- und mehrsilbige Adjektive,
- Adjektive, die auf *-ing* enden.

famous → more famous → most famous
boring → more boring → most boring

Achtung: Bei der Steigerung verändert sich oft die Schreibweise der Adjektive:
- Der Endkonsonant wird verdoppelt.
- Ein *-y* am Schluss wird durch *-i* ersetzt.
- Das stumme *-e* fällt weg.

hot → hotter → hottest
big → bigger → biggest
funny → funnier → funniest
angry → angrier → angriest
nice → nicer → nicest
close → closer → closest

Vergleicht man verschiedene Dinge oder Menschen, steht:
- Komparativ + **than** (Steigerung),
- **(not) as** + Adjektiv + **as** (Vergleich)

Ernie is **older than** (älter als) Ben.
This is **more important than** (wichtiger als) that.
This book is **as** cheap **as** (so billig wie) that CD.
Tina is not **as** intelligent **as** (nicht so intelligent wie) Peter.

WISSEN

5

Adjektive und Adverbien

ÜBUNG 1 Unterstreiche alle Adjektive, die sich hier verbergen.

(nice) – traffic – (terrible) – to walk – finger – (happy) – knee – wives – (short) – shelves – (expensive) – to laugh – dream – to hear – (soft) – (hard) – to find – tree – feeling – (cheap) – church – flower – to smell – tall – (big) – behind – after – to feel – (rich)

Handschriftliche Notizen: Datenverkehr, schrecklich, Ehefrauen, teuer, billig

ÜBUNG 2 Suche jeweils ein passendes Adjektiv zu einem Substantiv (Nomen). Schreibe die Lösungen, mit einem unbestimmten Artikel, in dein Übungsheft.

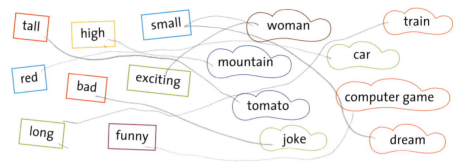

tall, high, small, woman, train, red, mountain, car, bad, exciting, computer game, long, funny, tomato, joke, dream

ÜBUNG 3 Stelle Vergleiche an. Schreibe jeweils zwei Sätze.

fast: plane – train

Planes are faster than trains. Trains are not as fast as planes.

high: Zugspitze – Mount Everest

Zugspitze are higher as Mount Everest

small: mouse – elephant

old: my granddad – my mum

difficult: maths – biology

expensive: computer – mobile phone

nice: my English teacher – my maths teacher

1.1 Adjektive

WISSEN

Unregelmäßig gesteigerte Adjektive
Unregelmäßige Formen haben:
gut: **good** → better → best
schlecht: **bad** → worse → worst

weit entfernt: **far** → farther / further → farthest / furthest

My bike is better than yours.
Today the weather is worse than yesterday.
London is farther away from New York than from Paris.

Mit *-er / -est* statt mit *more / most* werden die folgenden zweisilbigen Adjektive gesteigert:
klug: **clever** → cleverer → cleverest
ruhig: **quiet** → quieter → quietest
eng: **narrow** → narrower → narrowest

Randy is cleverer than we are, isn't he? – Yes, he is the cleverest boy in class.
Be careful! The road is narrower than I thought.

ÜBUNG 4 Hier darfst du mal richtig angeben. Steigere die Adjektive.

a friend:	you:	
My dad is rich.	My dad *is richer.*	
	He's the richest	person in the world.
My sister is beautiful.	My sister *is beautifuller*	
	She's the beautifullest	girl in the world.
I'm clever.	I'm *cleverer*	
		boy / girl in class.
My bike is fast.	My	
		bike in town.
I'm happy.	I'm	
		person on earth.
This film is good.	That	
		film ever.
My dog is really lazy.	My dog	
		dog in the world.
My brother is tall.	My brother	
		in our family.

Adjektive und Adverbien

> **WISSEN** ➕
>
> **Die Stellung der Adjektive**
> Attributiver Gebrauch: Wenn ein **Adjektiv** ein Substantiv näher beschreibt, steht es direkt **vor** dem Substantiv.
>
> The **little** <u>cat</u> is sitting on the **old** <u>tree</u>.
>
> ---
>
> **Prädikativer** Gebrauch: Das **Adjektiv** steht **nach** to be und **nach** den Verben
> to feel – sich fühlen, to look – aussehen,
> to sound – sich anhören, to smell – riechen,
> to taste – schmecken,
> wenn sie als Zustandsverben gebraucht werden.
>
> The girl <u>is</u> **nice**.
>
> He <u>feels</u> **happy**.
> She <u>looks</u> **sad**.
> The chips <u>taste</u> **good**.

 ÜBUNG 5   Bilde aus den folgenden Wörtern Sätze. Trage die Sätze in der richtigen Spalte ein und unterstreiche das Adjektiv.

chocolate / to like / the lady / young   Tim / sad / to look
big / the table / to be   she / to love / her ring / new
to feel / my friends / happy   cool / sunglasses / wearing / they're

attributiver Gebrauch	prädikativer Gebrauch
The <u>young</u> lady likes chocolate.	

 ÜBUNG 6   Übersetze die folgenden Sätze. Schreibe in dein Übungsheft.

Tina ist groß, aber Jenny ist größer. Jenny ist so groß wie Ben.
Sei vorsichtig! Du musst vorsichtiger sein als gestern.
Im April ist das Wetter schlecht, aber im November ist es schlechter.
Am schlechtesten ist es im Januar.
Ich bin so klug wie … *(Such dir jemanden aus!)*.

1.2 Adverbien der Art und Weise

Adverbien *(adverbs)* beschreiben eine Tätigkeit näher. Mit ihnen gibst du an, *wie* oder *auf welche Weise* man etwas macht.	He walks **slowly.** (*Wie* läuft er? Er läuft langsam.)
Adverbien bestimmen also ein Verb näher. Sie können jedoch auch ein Adjektiv genauer beschreiben.	Tim **works carefully.** (Das Verb wird näher bestimmt.) The book was **terribly boring.** (Das Adjektiv wird näher bestimmt.)
Das Adverb wird gebildet, indem man die Endung *-ly* an das Adjektiv hängt.	quiet → quietly nice → nicely
Aufgepasst: Einige Besonderheiten musst du beachten: ■ Endet das Adjektiv auf *-y*, wird die Adverbendung zu *-ily*. ■ Endet das Adjektiv auf *-le*, lautet die Adverbendung *-ly*. ■ Endet das Adjektiv auf *-ic*, ist die Adverbendung *-ically*.	happy → happily easy → easily simple → simply terrible → terribly basic → basically

Die Steigerung von Adverbien

Die meisten Adverbien auf *-ly* werden mit **more** und **most** gesteigert.	I write more carefully than my brother. But my mother writes most carefully.
Merke: Auch hier gibt es unregelmäßige Bildungen: *good (gut):* Adverb *well → better → best*	I can speak English very well, better than French.
bad (schlecht): Adverb *badly → worse → worst*	I slept badly last night, worse than last week.
Der Vergleich von Adverbien erfolgt wie bei den Adjektiven: ■ *(not) as* Adverb + *as* (Vergleich) ■ Komparativ oder Superlativ des Adverbs + *than*	I work **as** carefully **as** Simon. Ron doesn't work **as** carefully **as** Kim. Lizzy does her homework **more carefully than** her sister.

Adjektive und Adverbien

ÜBUNG 7 Unterstreiche in den Sätzen das Adverb.

My grandmother speaks quietly.

The pupils laughed loudly.

You can guess the answer easily.

She walked slowly out of the room.

Manchester United played badly and lost the match.

ÜBUNG 8 Bilde die Adverbform der Adjektive im Wortspeicher.

> loud – quiet – good – happy – careful – nervous – nice – lucky

ÜBUNG 9 Welches Adverb passt zu welchem Verb? Bilde jeweils einen einfachen Satz und schreibe die Sätze in dein Übungsheft.

Beispiel: Brad – write – carefully → Brad writes carefully.

| Mark – Simon – they – Peggy – I | shout – smile – drink – speak English – play soccer | angrily – happily – quickly – well – badly |

WISSEN

Verschiedene Arten von Adverbien
Neben den Adverbien der Art und Weise kennst du bereits weitere Adverbarten:
- Adverbien der Zeit: *Wann* passiert etwas?
- Adverbien des Ortes: *Wo* passiert etwas?
- Häufigkeitsadverbien: *Wie oft* geschieht etwas? (Stellung im Satz: ↑ S. 12)
- Gradadverbien: Sie verstärken eine Aussage oder schwächen sie ab.
- Satzadverbien: Sie beziehen sich auf den ganzen Satz.

I'm coming home **today**.

John is **outside**.

I **often** go shopping with my mum.

There was a lot of snow. I **almost** fell and broke my leg.

Of course I know the answer.

1.2 Adverbien der Art und Weise

ÜBUNG 10 Finde die acht Adverbien in dem Wortgitter. Achtung: Es verstecken sich auch ein Häufigkeitsadverb und ein Adverb der Zeit darin!

A	L	N	P	W	E	X	T	R	E	M	E	L	Y	V	I	Q	A	R
E	E	S	X	Z	J	P	L	K	O	T	G	C	S	D	Y	S	J	Z
B	A	G	J	Y	I	V	A	T	U	R	D	H	Z	R	T	A	B	X
F	S	K	W	M	O	X	Q	M	Y	H	S	F	C	D	O	C	X	W
H	I	L	E	N	G	R	H	A	P	P	I	L	Y	U	D	Z	L	B
M	L	R	L	F	B	F	E	E	G	E	T	C	D	K	A	M	B	L
T	Y	O	L	F	W	U	C	I	R	Q	B	A	D	L	Y	J	M	I
N	Q	E	H	P	V	P	J	N	S	E	P	B	D	U	V	N	O	Z
M	U	I	O	F	T	E	N	H	K	Q	H	F	X	O	W	C	G	A
L	A	D	K	K	T	J	I	O	C	A	R	E	F	U	L	L	Y	Y

ÜBUNG 11 Ergänze die Tabelle mit den richtigen Adverbformen.

to watch	carefully	more carefully	most carefully
to cycle	well		
to speak		more clearly	
to write		worse	
to speak	slowly		
to play volleyball			best
to talk		more loudly	

ÜBUNG 12 Wandle die Aussagen in Sätze mit Adverbien um. Das Verb des Satzes kannst du in der Regel aus der Personenbezeichnung ableiten.

Beispiel: James is a careful driver. → James drives carefully.

Betty is a perfect tennis player.
John is a nervous speaker.
They are careful readers.

Christy is a good dancer.
The rain is heavy in October.
My father is a fantastic cook.

Adjektive und Adverbien

ÜBUNG 13 Höre dir Track 1 auf der CD an und setze das passende Adverb ein. Achte auf Steigerungs- und Vergleichsformen!

Dear Peter,

How are you? I hope you are doing as _____ as I am. Let me tell you about a great day. Yesterday, I went to a birthday party. At the beginning I stood _____ alone because I didn't know anybody. But then some boys and girls came over and talked to me. We played badminton in the garden. I played _____ but the others played much _____. I was on a good team, so we won the match _____.
When it got dark, we made a bonfire (Lagerfeuer) _____. One of the boys played the guitar. We sang "Happy Birthday" _____ and started dancing _____. It was so much fun. But the best part of the evening was the fireworks at the end. Everyone watched _____ (aufgeregt).

Write back soon!

Yours, Mark

WISSEN

Die Stellung der Adverbien
Adverbien der Art und Weise stehen meist am Satzende.
Häufigkeitsadverbien stehen vor dem Verb.

Jeff opens the bag **slowly**.
Sandy listened to her mum **nervously**.
I **often** go skiing with my friends.
Sue **usually** tidies her room on Sundays.

ÜBUNG 14 Übersetze. Schreibe die Sätze in dein Übungsheft.

Ich gehe oft ins Kino.
Ich spreche gut Englisch.
Martin steht normalerweise um 7 Uhr auf.
Basketball spiele ich schlecht.

1.3 Adjektive und Adverbien im Vergleich

Adjektive und Adverbien bestimmen einen Satzteil (meist Substantiv und Verb) näher. Durch sie kannst du etwas genauer beschreiben.	It's summer and the sun is shining. → It's a very **hot** summer and the sun is shining **brightly.**
Adjektive beziehen sich auf Substantive oder Pronomen. Sie beschreiben, wie jemand oder etwas ist. **Adverbien** beziehen sich auf Verben oder Adjektive. Sie beschreiben, wie etwas getan wird oder wie sich etwas verhält.	Sam is happy. He's a happy boy. The mountain is high. It's a high mountain. Sam sings happily. The book is terribly exciting.
Merke: ■ Nach einem Zustandsverb (↑ S. 8) steht ein Adjektiv! ■ Nach einem Tätigkeitsverb steht ein Adverb!	Ron looks angry. → verärgert aussehen: ein Zustand Ron looks angrily at his teacher. → verärgert schauen: eine Tätigkeit

Besonderheiten bei der Adverbbildung

Es gibt eine Reihe von Adverbien, die die Form von Adjektiven haben: *early – früh* *late – spät* *fast – schnell* *long – lange* *high – hoch* *low – niedrig*	Susie is fast (Adjektiv). Susie runs fast (Adverb). I get up early and I go to bed late. Don't climb so high, it's dangerous.
Aufgepasst: Von einigen Adjektiven gibt es zwei Adverbformen, die unterschiedliche Bedeutung haben! *hard (hart)* ↔ *hardly (kaum)* *pretty (ziemlich)* ↔ *prettily (hübsch, schön)* *near (nahe)* ↔ *nearly (fast)*	Linda works hard. She hardly sleeps. Anna isn't only pretty clever, she also dresses prettily. Ben drove too near the river. He nearly had an accident.
Merke: Well kann nicht nur das Adverb von *good* sein, sondern auch ein eigenständiges Adjektiv! Es bedeutet dann *gesund.*	Ralph is ill. But he sleeps well (schläft gut), and soon he will be well (gesund) again.

Adjektive und Adverbien

ÜBUNG 15 Hier kannst du den Unterschied zwischen einem Satz mit Adjektiv und einem Satz mit Adverb gut erkennen. Setze das fehlende Wort ein.

happy	adjective:	Sam is happy .
	adverb:	Sam sings happily .
slow	adjective:	A VW Beetle is a car.
	adverb:	A VW Beetle driver drives .
sad	adjective:	It's a story.
	adverb:	He tells the story .
nervous	adjective:	Tim is very .
	adverb:	He talks .
quiet	adjective:	Lisa is a girl.
	adverb:	She talks .

ÜBUNG 16 Überlege, welche Adjektive und Adverbien hier passen könnten.

This is a   car. It drives   .

He's a   boy. He works   .

The basketball match is   . The players play

     .

ÜBUNG 17 Ersetze in den folgenden Sätzen die rot markierten Wörter duch die richtigen englischen Adjektiv- oder Adverbformen und schreibe die Sätze in dein Übungsheft.

My brother is (größer als) my sister.
The (alt) lady looks (ziemlich) (unglücklich).
It was the (schlimmster) day of my life: Someone stole my (neu) bike and I had a (schrecklich) toothache.
Computer games are (nicht so interessant wie) going on a (gefährlich) trip.
It was night. Teresa (kaum) saw anything.

1.3 Adjektive und Adverbien im Vergleich

ÜBUNG 18 Zustands- oder Tätigkeitsverb? Entscheide, ob du ein Adjektiv oder ein Adverb einsetzen musst.

The soup smells _____ (gut).
David has got a cold. He can't smell _____ (gut).
The fish tastes _____ (schlecht).
Marc tastes the meal _____ (vorsichtig).
George looks at his brother _____ (ärgerlich).
Linda isn't happy. She looks very _____ (ärgerlich).

ÜBUNG 19 Setze die richtige Form ein. Handelt es sich um ein Adjektiv oder ein Adverb?

A cheetah *(Gepard)* is a _____ (schnell) animal. A panther runs _____ (schnell), too.
Richard is a _____ (hart) worker. Susan works _____ (hart), too. But Tim _____ (kaum) works at all.
Anne is a _____ (hübsch) girl. She talks _____ (ziemlich) cool. And she laughs _____ (schön).
Marc is a _____ (gut) volleyball player. And Kim plays _____ (gut), too.

ÜBUNG 20 Übersetze.

Ich stehe jeden Tag früh auf.

Mein Vater fährt schneller als meine Mutter.

Rita sieht traurig aus. Sie fühlt sich schlecht.

Du sprichst gut Englisch.

Adjektive und Adverbien
Klassenarbeit 1

 45 Minuten

 AUFGABE 1 Finde das passende Adjektiv und die dazugehörigen Steigerungsformen.

Positiv	Komparativ	Superlativ
groß		
glücklich		
gefährlich		
gut		
schlecht		

 AUFGABE 2 Setze die Adjektive ein und verwandle sie in Adverbien.

Adjektiv	Adverb		Adjektiv	Adverb
vorsichtig		einfach		
furchtbar		fantastisch		
früh		schnell		

 AUFGABE 3 Lies den Text durch und unterstreiche Adjektive blau und Adverbien rot.

> Great fun and better marks
> Do you want to improve *(verbessern)* your English quickly and make new friends around the world? If yes, then join our interesting exchange programme *(Austauschprogramm)* and spend your holiday in beautiful Great Britain!
> You live comfortably with nice families. In the morning you'll study English in groups with friendly teachers. In the afternoons we'll take you on exciting trips. You'll visit important sights, take part in different sports activities, and meet new friends quickly. Isn't this the perfect way to learn English? If you are interested, please contact "Fun-Tours".

16

Klassenarbeiten

AUFGABE 4 Entscheide dich: Adjektiv oder Adverb?

Dear Lady Gaga,

My name is Gina and I am a _____ (big) fan of yours. I think you are very _____ (pretty) and that you dance _____ (beautiful). I would like to dance as _____ (good) as you. Last year I started dancing lessons. The instructor (Lehrer) is very _____ (strict) but I am getting _____ (good) _____ (quick).

My _____ (secret) wish is to dance _____ (professional) in one of your shows. How did you start your _____ (wonderful) career? Please give me some _____ (helpful) advice (Rat).

Your fan Gina

AUFGABE 5 Übersetze die Sätze. Achte auf die Satzstellung und alle Besonderheiten!

Richard öffnet seine Tasche langsam.
_____

Mein Vater ist ein vorsichtiger Fahrer.
_____

Es ist ein schneller Zug. Er fährt *(to travel)* sehr schnell.
_____

Betty ist ziemlich klug.
_____

Harry arbeitet sehr hart. Er schläft kaum.
_____

Jim tanzt sehr gut. Er ist ein guter Tänzer.
_____

Adjektive und Adverbien
Klassenarbeit 2

 60 Minuten

AUFGABE 6 Steigerung bei Adjektiven und Adverbien: Setze die fehlenden Formen ein.

good		
		most carefully
	worse	
		most terribly
	easier	
		greatest
slowly		
	narrower	
expensive		

AUFGABE 7 Setze die passende Form ein. Achte auf eventuelle Steigerungsformen!

Jenny feels _____ (besser als) yesterday but not _____ (gut) enough to go to school.

Sarah looked around _____ (nervös) and started to speak _____ (leise).

Jenny's mother opened the letter _____ (vorsichtig). It was a _____ (lang) letter with _____ (wunderschön) handwriting.

Mum drives _____ (schneller als) dad. She is not _____ (so vorsichtig wie) he is.

The police did a _____ (gut) job. They did their job very _____ (gut).

Klassenarbeiten

AUFGABE 8 Schreibe vollständige Sätze. Achte darauf, dass das Adjektiv an der richtigen Stelle im Satz steht.

Mr Smith / teacher / old

Los Angeles / city / famous

Robert Pattinson / actor / good-looking

Ants / animals / small

AUFGABE 9 Setze die angegebenen Adjektive in der richtigen Steigerungsform in die Lücke. Aufgepasst: Bei zwei Sätzen musst du den Superlativ verwenden.

Angelina Jolie is _____ (pretty) than our teacher.

My mum is _____ (young) than my friend's mum.

Mr Bond is _____ (handsome) than our neighbour.

The A 380 Airbus is _____ (big) passenger plane in the world.

My dad is _____ (strong) than me.

Our school is _____ (ugly) building in town.

A cat is _____ (intelligent) than a fish.

AUFGABE 10 Ordne die im Wortspeicher angegebenen Adverbien richtig zu.

there – slowly – today – lately – carefully – here – everywhere – already – happily – simply – outside – tomorrow – basically – badly

Art und Weise	Zeit	Ort

19

Adjektive und Adverbien

 AUFGABE 11 Adjektiv oder Adverb? Ergänze die Sätze.

It is not _____ (easy) to write a book.

Please remember to ride your bike _____ (careful). You often drive too _____ (quick).

My mum is very _____ (unhappy) because I don't write my homework _____ (tidy).

Dennis feels _____ (nervous) because he has a dentist's appointment in the afternoon.

The bus arrived _____ (late) again and so I missed the beginning of the show.

Pupils often think that they work _____ (hard) than their teachers.

 AUFGABE 12 Schreibe ganze Sätze. Achte darauf, die Adverbien an der richtigen Stelle im Satz zu platzieren (Ort vor Zeit!) und die richtige Zeit zu verwenden.

Peter / outside / to go / yesterday

Mr Smith / at the office / to arrive / at 8:30 a.m. / every weekday

You / to stop smoking / definitely / should

He / a lot / last week / to eat and to drink

 AUFGABE 13 Übersetze. Schreibe in dein Übungsheft.

Mein Vater spricht sehr schlecht Englisch.
Lilly spielt gut Cello.
Sie sangen das Geburtstagslied laut.
Sie wartete aufgeregt auf ihren Freund.
Das Essen riecht gut.
Mutter sieht ziemlich ärgerlich aus.

Modale Hilfsverben

2.1 Das Hilfsverb *können*

Die modalen Hilfsverben *can (können)* und *could* (Form im *simple past*) (↑ Kap. 3.2) stehen immer mit einem Vollverb.

Gina **can ride** a horse.
We **could go** to the cinema.
Can you ride a horse?

Mit *can* und *could* können auch Verneinungen und Fragen gebildet werden.

You **can't go** out now.
Couldn't you **come** earlier?

Aufgepasst: Can darf im Gegensatz zum Deutschen niemals allein stehen!

Ich kann Englisch. → I can speak English.

Das Hilfsverb *can* drückt aus:
◼ eine Fähigkeit oder Unfähigkeit,
◼ eine Erlaubnis oder ein Verbot,
◼ eine Bitte,
◼ eine Möglichkeit oder Unmöglichkeit.

I can speak French. / I can't help you.
You can park here. / You can't park here.
Can I get your pen?
That can't be Mrs Cooper.

Das Hilfsverb *could* bezeichnet
◼ die Vergangenheitsform *(konnte)*,
◼ eine höfliche Frage *(könnte)*.

My grandfather could speak Greek.
Could you pass me the sugar, please?

Aufgepasst: Can und *could* sind nur im *simple present* und im *simple past* verwendbar. Für alle anderen Zeiten brauchst du die **Ersatzform**

simple present: I can ride a bike.
simple past: He could not find his pen.

to be able to (können, fähig sein).

Merke: Can/could bezeichnet eine allgemeine Fähigkeit, *to be able to* bezieht sich auf eine spezielle Situation.

will-future: He won't be able to repair his car.
I can swim very fast. I am able to break the school record.

Die verneinten Formen lauten:
can → *cannot* (Kurzform *can't*)
could → *could not* (Kurzform *couldn't*)
to be able to → *to be not able to*

I can't open the door.
He couldn't do his homework.
He wasn't able to open the door.

Modale Hilfsverben

 ÜBUNG 1 Was kannst du, was nicht? Was ist erlaubt, was nicht? Schreibe in dein Übungsheft.

Beispiel: to play / the guitar / the trumpet → I can play the guitar. I cannot / can't play the trumpet.

to ride / a horse / an elephant
to speak / English / Chinese
to repair / a bike / a car
to go / to Italy / to the moon
to drink lemonade / beer

 ÜBUNG 2 Setze *can, cannot, could* oder *could not* ein.

_____ you give me the book, please?

Thomas and Tina _____ do a lot of tricks.

When I was young I _____ walk on my hands.

I _____ do it now.

You can take my old bike. But you _____ use my new bike.

King Edward I lived from 1239 – 1307. He _____ speak different languages. But he _____ use a computer. They had no computers around 1300.

 ÜBUNG 3 Setze die passende Form des englischen Hilfsverbs *können* in die Lücke. Wenn es mehrere Möglichkeiten gibt (Ersatzform!), trage alle ein. Achte auf die Zeiten!

Last year we _____ go to India.

At the moment Marc _____ (not) play the guitar. But he has got a teacher now. Next year he _____ (will-future) play the guitar.

Toby _____ (not) ride a bike when he was three.

But now he's twelve, so he _____ ride a bike.

_____ to climb Mount Everest?

22

2.2 Das Hilfsverb *dürfen*

Wenn man eine Erlaubnis ausdrücken möchte, kann man ebenfalls *can* benutzen. Allerdings muss man in allen Zeiten – außer im *simple present* – die **Ersatzform** **to be allowed to** *(dürfen)* verwenden.	*simple present:* Jane can / is allowed to come. *simple past:* She was allowed to come. *will-future:* She will be allowed to come.
Die **Verneinung** wird mit *not* gebildet und drückt ein Verbot aus: *to be not allowed to (nicht dürfen)*	Jane is not allowed to go to Peter's party tonight. She wasn't allowed to come. She won't be allowed to come.
Wenn man eine höfliche Frage stellen will, verwendet man statt *can* das Hilfsverb **may**.	May we (könnten / dürften wir) have a cup of tea, please? May I go to the concert?
May (not) kann auch ein Verbot oder eine Erlaubnis ausdrücken. Es ist formeller als *can*.	Tourists may use the swimming pool from 9 a.m. till 5 p.m. Guests may not smoke. Visitors may not walk on the grass in public gardens.
Das Hilfsverb *may (might)* wird auch verwendet, um eine Vermutung auszudrücken.	He might be sick. Jane might buy a new dress für Linda's party.
Neben der allgemeinen Verneinungsform *to be not allowed to* wird eine weitere Form der Verneinung mit **mustn't** gebildet. Sie bezeichnet ein strenges Verbot (↑ Kap. 2.3).	Ben mustn't watch (darf nicht) TV in the evenings. You mustn't steal your brother's toys! You mustn't drive a car! You haven't got a licence *(Führerschein)*.

Modale Hilfsverben

 ÜBUNG 4 Verwende *to be (not) allowed to*. Schreibe die Sätze in dein Übungsheft.

to go swimming	✓	to watch the show	✗
to run fast	✗	to do the washing-up	✓
to sing a love song	✓	to watch a film on TV	✓
to play a computer game	✗	to go to the party	✗

WISSEN ➕

Modale Hilfsverben wie *can, could, may, must* stehen immer mit einem Vollverb (ohne *to*). *Merke:* Sie haben in der 3. Person Singular Präsens kein *-s*.	I can hear music. You may use the bathroom. I must get up. He can help me.
Primäre Hilfsverben sind *to be*, *to have*, *to do*. Wie die modalen Hilfsverben bilden auch sie Fragen, Verneinungen und Zeiten.	He is cleaning the window. Kim hasn't been here for two years. Did you like the concert?

 ÜBUNG 5 Höre dir Track 2 auf der CD an und setze die fehlenden Formen ein. Achte auch auf Signalwörter, die dir Hinweise auf die richtige Zeitform geben.

You _____ turn left (Verbot), but you _____ (Erlaubnis) turn right.

_____ (höfliche Frage) I help you with your work?

She _____ (Verbot) borrow *(leihen)* the skateboard last week.

_____ (you, Erlaubnis) watch TV last week?

Dogs _____ in the cinema (Verbot).

You _____ (starkes Verbot) bring your dog.

Visitors _____ (höflich formuliertes Verbot) use their mobile phones during the show.

 ÜBUNG 6 Übersetze die folgenden Sätze. Schreibe in dein Übungsheft.

Jane durfte uns besuchen.
Tom wird nicht bleiben dürfen.
Darf er mit uns kommen?

2.3 Das Hilfsverb *müssen*

Das Hilfsverb *must* bezeichnet ■ eine Notwendigkeit und Verpflichtung, ■ eine Gewissheit, ■ eine Schlussfolgerung oder ■ eine Aufforderung.	I must go now. Tim must be tired. He stayed up long. It's 2 o'clock now. School must be over. You must be quiet now.
Ersatzformen für *must* sind *need* und *have (got) to.* Die deutsche **Verneinung** *muss nicht / braucht nicht* wird im Englischen nur mit den **Ersatzformen** *do not have to (don't have to)* oder *need not (needn't)* gebildet.	I **must** go now. I **need to** go now. I **have to** go now. I**'ve got to** go now. We **don't have to** go to the cinema. / We **need not** go to the cinema. (Wir müssen nicht ins Kino gehen. / Wir brauchen nicht ins Kino zu gehen.)
Für die **anderen Zeiten** brauchst du ebenfalls die Ersatzform *have to* (müssen), da du *must* und *needn't* nur in der Gegenwart verwenden kanns.	I must tidy my room today. → I had to tidy my room yesterday. You needn't do your homework. → You will not (won't) have to do your homework tomorrow.
Aufgepasst: Bildest du eine **Verneinung** oder eine **Frage** mit der Ersatzform *have to*, musst du das Hilfsverb *to do* verwenden.	Do you have to get up early? No, I don't have to get up early.
Im *simple past* nimmst du statt *do* die Form *did*.	Did she have to work last week? – No, she didn't have to work last week.
Achtung: Zwischen *must* und *have to* gibt es einen Bedeutungsunterschied: ■ *must* drückt ein **persönliches Bedürfnis** aus, ■ *have to* bezeichnet einen **äußeren Zwang**.	I am hungry. I must eat something. I have to go shopping. My mother told me to.
Merke: must heißt *müssen*, *mustn't* heißt *nicht dürfen*!	You must tell the truth. You mustn't eat all the cookies.

Modale Hilfsverben

 ÜBUNG 7 Pits Mutter sagt Pit, was er alles zu tun hat. Setze in den gelben Feldern *must* und das passende Verb ein.

Mum: "Pit, after school you _____ your bike! Then you _____. You _____ it to your father in the evening. At 5 o'clock you _____. And at 9 o'clock you _____. You _____ early tomorrow!"

 ÜBUNG 8 Am nächsten Tag erzählt Pit seinen Freunden, was er gestern alles tun musste. Schreibe den Text aus Übung 7 in dein Übungsheft. Setze das *simple past* von *to have to* ein.
Achtung: Statt *you / your* brauchst du nun *I / my*!
Beginne folgendermaßen: Pit: "After school I had to clean my bike."

 ÜBUNG 9 Achte auf den Bedeutungsunterschied: *must* (persönliches Bedürfnis) oder *to have to* (äußerer Zwang)?

My teacher is very strict *(streng)*. I _____ do my homework.

I have been running for one hour. I _____ drink something.

Mother to Jill: "Don't be late! You _____ be home at 10 o'clock!" – Jill to her friends: "I _____ be home at 10. My mother told me so."

2.3 Das Hilfsverb *müssen*

WISSEN

Fragen und Verneinungen
Fragen und Verneinungen werden bei den modalen Hilfsverben direkt mit dem Hilfsverb gebildet – nicht mit *to do* (außer bei *to have to*). Beachte die Wortstellung in den Beispielen.

Can I help you? – No, you cannot help me.
May I turn the light off? – No, you may not turn the light off.
Were you able to find it? – No, we were not able to find it.
Am I allowed to come in? – No, you are not allowed to come in.

ÜBUNG 10 Bilde die richtigen Fragen und Verneinungen.

to be allowed to – you / go *(simple past)*:

<u>Were you allowed to go to</u> the party? –
No, I <u>wasn't allowed to go to the party</u> .

can – we / help *(simple present)*:

_____ you, sir? –
No, you _____ .

to be allowed to – he / take *(simple present)*:

_____ this bike? –
No, he _____ .

may – I / have:

_____ a bottle of coke, please? –
No, you _____ .

to be allowed to – she / call *(will-future)*:

_____ me tomorrow? –
No, she _____ tomorrow.

to be able to – you / repair *(simple past)*:

_____ the fridge? –
No, we _____ .

Can – you / see *(simple present)*:

_____ the moon? – No, I _____ .

Modale Hilfsverben

WISSEN +

Achtung Verwechslungsgefahr!
Don't have to, *needn't* und *mustn't* sind leicht zu verwechseln. Präge dir den Unterschied ein:
nicht müssen – *don't have to*
nicht brauchen – *needn't*
nicht dürfen – *mustn't*

Du **musst** das **nicht** tun. – You **don't have to** do that.
Du **brauchst** das **nicht** zu tun. – You **needn't** do that.
Du **darfst** das **nicht** tun. – You **mustn't** do that.

 ÜBUNG 11 Fülle die Lücken mit der passenden Form von *to have to*. Achte auf die Signalwörter für die Vergangenheit und für das *will-future*. Achtung: An zwei Stellen musst du eine Frage formulieren!

A three-day snowboard course

Instructor: "Good morning everyone. How do you feel after your first day of snowboarding?"

Betty: "I feel good today but I _____ go to bed early yesterday. I was so tired."

Instructor: "That's alright. On your first day you _____ learn all the basics *(Grundlagen)*. Today we will practise *(üben)* a lot. Remember, tomorrow you _____ pass a test. So we _____ start right away *(sofort)*."

John: "Can we put on our snowboards right now? Or _____ have a warming-up first?"

Instructor: "Of course, you always _____ do a warming-up first. Today you _____ get up the hill with the lift. To use the lift – what _____ do?"

Steven: "We _____ stand on the snowboard with one foot only."

Instructor: "You're right. Good luck – I will see you on top of the hill."

2.3 Das Hilfsverb *müssen*

ÜBUNG 12 Überlege, ob du *mustn't*, *needn't* oder *don't have to* einsetzen musst. Übersetze nur die roten Satzteile.

Du musst nicht in die Schule gehen.

Du brauchst mir nicht zu helfen, ich komme allein zurecht.

Du darfst nicht zu viel trinken, du bekommst sonst Bauchweh.

Ihr braucht nicht zu bezahlen, ich lade euch ein.

Du musst heute nicht früh ins Bett gehen.

Ich darf heute nicht lange aufbleiben *(stay up)*.

ÜBUNG 13 Im Englischunterricht kann man die modalen Hilfsverben gut verwenden. Wie lauten die richtigen Sätze? Höre dir dazu Track 3 auf der CD an. (Hinweis: Bei einigen Sätzen gibt es zwei Möglichkeiten.)

Du bittest deinen Lehrer, etwas zu wiederholen *(repeat)*: "Can you repeat it, please?"

Du musst jetzt gehen: "I   now."

Dein Lehrer braucht dir nicht helfen: "You   ."

Ist es möglich, das Fenster zu öffnen: "   the window?"

Du konntest gestern keine Hausaufgaben machen: "I   yesterday."

Du möchtest eine Frage stellen: "   ?"

Der Lehrer sagt, dass ihr leise sein müsst: "You   ."

29

Modale Hilfsverben
Klassenarbeit 1

⏱ 45 Minuten

 AUFGABE 1 Verbinde die einzelnen Sätze mit der passenden Bedeutung durch eine Linie.

May I have a glass of water, please?	Fähigkeit
The bus mustn't stop here.	Möglichkeit
You can do your homework later.	striktes Verbot
You must be careful.	Erlaubnis
Willy was able to dance.	höfliche Bitte
Are we allowed to listen?	Aufforderung

 AUFGABE 2 Bilde entsprechende Sätze im *simple present* und der 2. Person Singular (du). Achtung: Manchmal gibt es zwei Möglichkeiten!

nicht dürfen: to sit here

You

müssen: to wear a helmet *(Helm)*

You

höfliche Bitte: to help you *(Frage!)*

nicht müssen: to wait for me

You

nicht brauchen: to do the washing-up

You

dürfen: to watch the film

You

können: to speak Chinese *(Frage!)*

Klassenarbeiten

AUFGABE 3 Fit in allen Zeiten? Setze die Sätze in die angegebene Zeitform. Achte darauf, immer die Ersatzformen zu verwenden, und schreibe ganze Sätze.

1. Tom can ride a motor bike.
   simple past:
   will-future:

2. She must write a story.
   simple past:
   will-future:

3. I can go camping with my friends. (Erlaubnis!)
   simple past:
   will-future:

4. Richard and Diana needn't come.
   simple past:
   will-future:

AUFGABE 4 Übersetze die rot markierten Satzteile. Schreibe in dein Übungsheft.

Ich durfte leider nicht fernsehen.
Musstet ihr gestern lange warten?
Wir konnten die Flasche nicht öffnen.
Wirst du morgen bei der Aufführung singen können?

AUFGABE 5 Bilde Fragen und Verneinungen. Achte dabei auf die Zeiten! Schreibe die Sätze in dein Übungsheft.

Musstet ihr gestern arbeiten?
Wirst du morgen kommen können?
Laila braucht nicht ins Bett zu gehen.
Darf ich dir eine Frage stellen?
Durfte Dean zuhören?
Vera darf nicht kommen.
Muss sie Tee trinken?

Modale Hilfsverben
Klassenarbeit 2

 45 Minuten

 AUFGABE 6 Setze die Hilfsverben *can*, *must* und *may* in der angegebenen Person in die richtige Form. Nenne, wo es möglich ist, immer auch die Ersatzformen.

can → 1. Person Singular *simple present*

can → 3. Person Plural *simple past*

may → 2. Person Singular *future*

may → 1. Person Plural *simple past*

must → 1. Person Singular *simple past*

must → 2. Person Plural *future*

 AUFGABE 7 Wer kann was? Schreibe vollständige Sätze in dein Übungsheft.

Beispiel: Mary / play the violin / swim → Mary can play the violin and can swim, but she can't ride a unicycle or do karate.

	play the violin	ride a unicycle (Einrad)	swim	do karate
Mary	✓	–	✓	–
Peter	–	–	✓	✓
Jamie	✓	✓	✓	–
Helena	–	✓	✓	–
Vicky	–	–	–	✓
Robin	–	–	✓	–

Klassenarbeiten

AUFGABE 8 *To have to, to be allowed to, to be able to?* **Setze das richtige Hilfsverb in die Lücke.**

Do you want to see a movie tonight? I'd really like, but I can't. I _____ study for my math exam.

Did you go to school yesterday? No, I didn't. I was ill and _____ stay in bed. I _____ get up and watch TV.

I went shopping yesterday. I really _____ buy a new pair of jeans because I tore my favourite jeans in a bike accident.

My leg is broken. I _____ do any sports for four weeks.

Mother to her daughter: You _____ go to that party next weekend if you help me tidy up the kitchen.

May I smoke? No, you _____ smoke inside here. This is a non-smoking building.

I can't go out tonight. I _____ finish my essay.

AUFGABE 9 *Must, mustn't, needn't?* **Setze das richtige Hilfsverb in die Lücke.**

You _____ have a passport when you travel to the USA.
You _____ exchange Euro money when you travel to Slovakia.
You _____ be late for school.
You _____ smoke inside this building.

AUFGABE 10 Übersetze. Schreibe in dein Übungsheft.

Ich spreche Französisch. Kann ich Ihnen helfen?
Wir könnten ins Kino gehen.
Jane darf nicht auf Peters Party gehen.
Ich muss heute mein Zimmer aufräumen.
Ich musste gestern mein Zimmer aufräumen.
I habe wirklich Hunger. Ich muss jetzt etwas essen.
Vor Gericht *(in court)* musst du die Wahrheit sagen.

3 Vergangenheit

3.1 Das *simple past*

Im Englischen benutzt man für die abgeschlossene Vergangenheit das *simple past*.	Last week Mr Harris **was** in hospital. I **had** an accident yesterday.
Verwende das *simple past*, wenn ■ eine Handlung zu einem bestimmten Zeitpunkt in der Vergangenheit liegt und abgeschlossen ist, ■ mehrere Handlungen in der Vergangenheit aufeinander folgten und nun abgeschlossen sind.	Ryan was ill last Monday (→ jetzt ist er wieder gesund). We had a party two weeks ago (→ sie ist längst vorüber). We went home, had dinner and drank a cup of coffee.
Bei folgenden **Signalwörtern** musst du immer das *simple past* verwenden: *yesterday* – gestern *last week / last month / last year* – letzte Woche / letzter Monat / letztes Jahr *... ago* – vor ... *in* + Jahreszahl – Jahreszahl	I was at home **yesterday.** **Last summer** she met Susan. **Three years ago** we were in Spain. **In 2012** the Olympic Games were in London.

Das *simple past* bei regelmäßigen Verben

Es gibt **regelmäßige** und **unregelmäßige** Verben. Das *simple past* von regelmäßigen Verben bildest du so: Grundform des Verbs (ohne *to*) + *-ed*	rain + -ed → rained talk + -ed → talked ask + -ed → asked
Achte hier auf die **Schreibung:** ■ Steht ein *-e* am Wortende, wird nur ein *-d* hinzugefügt, ■ Konsonant + *-y* wird zu *-ied,* ■ betonter Einzelvokal + Konsonant am Ende führen zur Konsonantenverdopplung.	to live → lived, to phone → phoned to try → tried, to worry → worried to stop → stopped, to spot → spotted

WISSEN

34

3.1 Das *simple past*

ÜBUNG 1   Setze die richtige Verbform im *simple past* ein.

Two thousand years ago,

people _____ (to live) differently.

They _____ (to own) no cars and

_____ (to use) no mobile phones.

They _____ (to talk) about different

things and _____ (to like) different clothes.

ÜBUNG 2   Schreibe alle regelmäßigen *simple past*-Formen aus der Wortschlange in dein Übungsheft.

torungoodwashedtodrinkplayedhousebehind
telephonelikedlovestayedsong
watchedopenedyesenteredtoseephoned

WISSEN ➕

Aussprache
Aufgepasst: Die *simple past*-Formen werden verschieden ausgesprochen:
- Nach Vokal und stimmhaftem Konsonant folgt [d],
- nach stimmlosem Konsonant folgt [t],
- nach [d] oder [t] folgt [ɪd].

phoned [fəʊnd], stayed [steɪd]

worked [wɜːkt], helped [helpt]
waited [ˈweɪtɪd], wanted [ˈwɒntɪd]

ÜBUNG 3   Bilde die richtige *simple past*-Form. Schreibe die Aussprache der Endung der *simple past*-Form in eckige Klammer.

to phone →	phoned [d]	to want →	wanted [ɪd]
to worry →		to tidy →	
to work →		to arrive →	
to stop →		to live →	
to wait →		to like →	

35

Vergangenheit

 ÜBUNG 4 Unterstreiche in dem folgenden Brief die *simple past*-Formen der regelmäßigen Verben.

Dear Bill,
Last week I travelled from Germany to London with my class. We saw a lot of buildings and places, and on our last day we visited Madame Tussaud's, the wax figure museum. We looked at all the wax figures of famous (berühmt) people, for example the Queen, Madonna, and Michael Jackson. We had our cameras with us and had a lot of fun. When we entered another room, somebody shouted: "Elvis lives!" We turned around and could see the Elvis figure. We were very frightened because suddenly Elvis started to move and play the guitar. When the shock was over, we started to laugh: It was just a joke – we noticed that Elvis was just an actor.
Hope to hear from you soon!
Yours, Peter

 ÜBUNG 5 Trage nun alle regelmäßigen *simple past*-Formen in die Tabelle ein (ohne Dopplungen) und leite den passenden Infinitiv mit *to* ab.

simple past	Grundform mit *to*	simple past	Grundform mit *to*

 ÜBUNG 6 Letztes Wochenende hatten Susan und Toby viel zu tun. Bilde Sätze im *simple past*. Schreibe sie in dein Übungsheft.

Susan / to water / the flowers.
Toby / to tidy *(aufräumen)* / his room.
Susan and Toby / to clean / the kitchen.
Toby / to repair / his bike.
Susan / to play / with the dogs.
Susan / to work / with her father.
They / to watch / TV / in the evening.

3.2 Das *simple past* bei unregelmäßigen Verben

Für die Bildung des *simple past* bei unregelmäßigen Verben gibt es keine festen Regeln. Daher musst du dir die Formen genau einprägen und am besten auswendig lernen.	to do → did I did the washing-up. to write → wrote Ricky wrote a letter.
Eine Zusammenstellung der wichtigsten unregelmäßigen Verben findest du auf S. 52.	to get → got Tina got a letter.
Für die Bildung des *simple past* verwendet man die 2. Verbform.	to forget → forgot Tina forgot her brother's birthday.
Bei einigen Verben sind verschiedene *simple past*-Formen möglich, verwenden darfst du beide:	
to learn → learned / learnt (lernen)	Last year I learned to play tennis.
to dream → dreamed / dreamt (träumen)	Last night I dreamt of you.
Die *simple past*-Formen der wichtigsten **Modalverben** lauten: *can → could* *must → had to* *needn't → didn't have to*	Last night I couldn't sleep. I had to do my homework before dinner. I didn't have to be home before dinner.
Bei einigen Verben wird die Verbform im *simple past* **nicht verändert**: *to cost → cost (kosten)* *to cut → cut (schneiden)* *to hit → hit (schlagen)* *to hurt → hurt (verletzen)* *to let → let (lassen)* *to put → put (setzen, stellen, legen)*	The CDs cost (kosten / kosteten) twenty pounds. I cut (schneide / schnitt) the bread with a knife. I let (lasse / ließ) the dog out. They put (stellen / stellten) the books onto the shelf.
Achtung: Beim Verb *to read* ändert sich beim Übergang ins *simple past* zwar nicht die Schreibung, aber die Aussprache: *to read [riːd] → read [red] (lesen)*	Tim read an interesting book last week.

Vergangenheit

Das *simple past* von *to be* und *to have*

Das unregelmäßige Verb **to be** hat im *simple past* die beiden Formen **was** und **were:**

Singular:
I was
you were
he / she / it was

I was happy.
Were you in school yesterday?
She was lazy.

Plural:
we were
you were
they were

On Sunday we were in town.
You were very brave, girls!
They were happy

Das unregelmäßige Verb **to have** wird im *simple past* zu **had.** Es bleibt in allen Personalformen gleich.

I had a headache yesterday.
Last year she had short hair.
We had fun at the party.

Fragen und Verneinungen im *simple past*

Fragen in der Vergangenheit werden in der Regel mit *did* gebildet, der *simple past*-Form des unregelmäßigen Hilfsverbs *to do.*

Did you lose your keys?

Didn't she look great yesterday?

Bei **Verneinungen** benötigst du die verneinte Form von *did*, also *did not/didn't*, sowie die Grundform des Vollverbs.

Tom sold his bike, but he did not/didn't sell his game boy.

Merke: Das *simple past* wird bereits durch das *did* angezeigt, daher steht das folgende Vollverb in der Grundform (Infinitiv ohne *to*).

Fragen und Verneinungen im *simple past* kannst du ausführlicher auch im Kapitel 6.1 üben.

3.2 Das *simple past* bei unregelmäßigen Verben

ÜBUNG 7   Finde die 12 unregelmäßigen *simple past*-Formen im Wortgitter, trage sie in dein Übungsheft ein und schreibe jeweils rechts daneben die Grundform.

U	P	A	T	S	U	O	S	N	M	B	Y	C	A	Z
L	V	W	B	U	I	L	T	I	H	J	G	B	Y	B
V	Q	K	R	S	X	N	O	L	J	D	D	O	K	E
X	D	Y	R	B	T	W	O	X	C	R	B	U	F	A
F	R	E	Q	F	D	E	D	J	H	E	Z	G	Z	L
H	A	Z	C	M	W	D	L	K	H	W	V	H	P	M
G	N	A	P	R	O	D	E	C	G	B	O	T	S	Y
O	K	I	Q	W	J	F	K	V	I	X	R	N	U	U
R	N	D	G	N	C	O	U	L	D	P	Q	O	F	A
E	V	S	P	M	L	C	O	X	R	Q	G	B	D	T
Y	T	K	N	E	W	N	D	O	Y	T	A	C	I	Z
U	U	M	M	K	O	E	W	S	R	A	V	B	D	E
Z	A	N	L	X	T	G	W	R	O	T	E	T	C	S
V	F	O	U	N	D	H	G	I	J	F	G	Z	D	A
J	K	K	F	L	I	J	S	M	F	E	Q	D	F	R

ÜBUNG 8   Bilde wie im Beispiel aus den Satzteilen Fragen und beantworte sie dann einmal bejaht und einmal verneint. Schreibe in dein Übungsheft.

Beispiel: Did they come to the party? → Yes, they came to the party. / No, they didn't come to the party.

- to go to the shop – they
- to lose her purse – Tina
- ~~come to the party – they~~
- to clean the room – they
- to drink a milk shake – you
- to buy a book – Sandra

ÜBEN

39

Vergangenheit

ÜBUNG 9 Übersetze die folgenden Sätze. Schreibe sie in dein Übungsheft.

1. Tom und Tina waren glücklich.
2. Meine Familie hatte einen großen Hund.
3. Es war sehr lustig.
4. Gestern waren wir zu Hause.
5. Er hatte eine Erkältung.
6. Letzten Montag war ich krank.
7. Letzten Sommer arbeitete Frank im Zoo.

ÜBUNG 10 In Marys Tagebuch fehlen die richtigen Verbformen. Höre dir Track 4 auf der CD an und fülle die Lücken mit der passenden *simple past*-Form der Verben im Wortspeicher. Überprüfe anschließend dein Ergebnis, in dem du dir nochmals Track 4 anhörst.

4

> to do – to visit – to have to – to have – to know – to be – to be –
> to be – to help – to get up – to give – to run – cannot – not to have to –
> to play – to go – to go – to have – to buy – to eat – to write –
> to drink – to watch – to wake up

On Monday, I _____ my friend Susan. She _____ ill. I _____ her with her homework, but she _____ all the answers herself (selbst). Her mother _____ us some drinks and some sandwiches. In the evening, I _____ Monopoly with my brother. I _____ to bed early, but I _____ sleep. On Tuesday, I _____ to see the dentist (Zahnarzt) because I _____ some problems with my teeth. After that my mother _____ me a new shirt. On Wednesday, I _____ an English test. In the afternoon I _____ my homework. Then I _____ some chocolate and _____ some tea. In the evening, I _____ a film about Africa. On Thursday, I _____ at 7:30 a.m. I _____ late, so I _____ to school. I really _____ hurry! On Friday, I _____ go to school because our teacher _____ ill. She _____ a bad cold, just like Susan on Monday. So I _____ at 10 a.m.

40

3.3 Das *past progressive*

Die Bildung des *past progressive*

Im Englischen gibt es für das *simple present* eine Verlaufsform, das *present progressive*. Das Gleiche gilt für das *simple past*: Seine Verlaufsform heißt *past progressive*.	The phone rings. The phone **is ringing**. They listened to music. They **were listening** to music.
So bildest du das *past progressive*: *was / were* + Infinitiv (ohne *to*) + *-ing*	It was raining. They were doing the dishes.

Die Verwendung des *past progressive*

Das *past progressive* drückt aus, dass eine Handlung in der Vergangenheit gerade im Verlauf und zum damaligen Zeitpunkt noch nicht abgeschlossen war.	I was playing football when my mum called me to dinner The birds were singing in the trees.
Du verwendest das *past progressive*, wenn ■ du den **Ablauf** einer Handlung betonen möchtest, der einen ganzen Zeitraum ausfüllte, ■ eine **Handlung ablief** (Hintergrundhandlung), während eine weitere (vergangene) Handlung im *simple past* einsetzte.	He was writing letters from 7 till 10. She was watching TV when the bell rang. I woke up because the phone was ringing.

Vergleich *simple past* und *past progressive*

past progressive: ■ Handlungsabläufe in einem bestimmten Zeitraum, ■ eine bereits andauernde Handlung („Hintergrundhandlung")	I was cleaning my bike all Sunday morning. I was dancing in the room when somebody knocked at the door.
simple past: ■ Einzelhandlungen, die abgeschlossen sind, ■ aufeinander folgende Handlungen	Jane wrote an e-mail. She went shopping, then she met Ann.

Vergangenheit

 ÜBUNG 11 Die folgenden Sätze beinhalten *simple past* und *past progressive*. Unterstreiche das *simple past* in Rot und das *past progressive* in Blau.

Last Sunday we had dinner. After dinner we played a game and talked about the day. We went to bed early.

While we were listening to the concert, they stole my bike.

His friends were waiting in the kitchen while Tom was cleaning his room.

 ÜBUNG 12 Was passiert auf den Bildern? Bilde Sätze mit der *past progressive*-Form.

Sandra _____ .

 Tina _____ .

Rick _____ .

 They _____ .

Tim _____ .

 Sarah and Jane _____ .

WISSEN ➕

Signalwörter für das *past progressive*
Hintergrundhandlungen werden oft mit *while* (während) eingeleitet. Für die plötzlich einsetzende Handlung im *simple past* kann *when* (als) verwendet werden.

Achtung: In einem Satz darf immer nur eins von beiden stehen! *While* kann auch für zwei gleichzeitig ablaufende Handlungen eingesetzt werden.

while + past progressive:
While Francis **was waiting** for the bus, it started to rain.
Anna **was having** dinner **while** Charles **was cleaning** the kitchen.

when + simple past:
When the strange man **entered** the room, everybody was talking.

3.3 Das *past progressive*

ÜBUNG 13   Fülle die Lücken mit der richtigen Zeitform – *past progressive* oder *simple past?*

I _____ (to eat) a sandwich when the phone _____ (to ring).

When Tina _____ (to enter) the restaurant, her family

_____ (to wait) there.

While they _____ (to sit) in the waiting room, the door

_____ (to open) and an old lady _____ (to come) in.

Mum _____ (to come) home while I _____ (to play) with

our dog.

Ryan _____ (to sleep) when Mr Miller _____ (to call).

ÜBUNG 14   Die Satzteile stehen in der richtigen Reihenfolge. Bilde daraus zusammen-
hängende Sätze mit der richtigen Zeit und schreibe sie in dein Übungsheft.

while / Kitty / to have / a shower / Marc / to come / home
I / to play / volleyball / when / Harry / to tell / me / the news
George and Emily / to laugh / when / the taxi / to arrive
The boys / to play / football / while / the girls / to skate / in the park
Mr Stevenson / to talk / to his friend / when / he / to see / the accident

ÜBUNG 15   Übersetze.

Mr Miller ging über die Straße, als der Unfall passierte.

Während sie im Garten spielte, begann es zu regnen.

Tom und Philipp machten Hausaufgaben, während Mrs Jones kochte.

Ich schrieb gerade einen Brief an Oma, als der Briefträger *(postman)* an der Tür
klingelte.

43

3.4 Das *present perfect*

Das einfache Perfekt (*present perfect*) beschreibt eine Handlung oder ein Ereignis, das bis in die Gegenwart andauert oder hineinwirkt.	The Smiths **have lived** here for five years (→ sie leben immer noch hier). Eve **has** just **eaten** a sandwich (→ sie ist jetzt satt). Greg **has opened** the window (→ das Fenster ist jetzt offen).

Das *present perfect* bei regelmäßigen Verben

So wird das *present perfect* mit regelmäßigen Verben gebildet: *have / has + past participle* (3. Verbform)	Marc and John have played volleyball for two hours now. Judy has played the piano since 5 o'clock.
Das *past participle* bei regelmäßigen Verben ist das Partizip der Vergangenheit und wird wie die *simple past*-Form der regelmäßigen Verben gebildet (↑ Kap. 3.1).	to walk → walked → has / have walked to call → called → has / have called to jump → jumped → has / have jumped

Das *present perfect* bei unregelmäßigen Verben

Wie im *simple past* gibt es auch im *present perfect* unregelmäßige Verbformen, für die es keine festen Regeln gibt. Präge sie dir gut ein und lerne sie auswendig. Eine Übersicht über die wichtigsten unregelmäßigen Verben findest du auf Seite 52!	to do → done I have done everything. to write → written My father has written a letter to grandma. to eat → eaten Gina has just eaten the cake. to go → gone I have gone to school for six years now.
Die *present perfect*-Form des **Hilfsverbs** *must* lautet *have had to*.	I have had to do the shopping.
Achtung: Von dem Hilfsverb *can* gibt es keine *present perfect*-Form! Du musst die Ersatzform von *to be able to – können / to be allowed to – dürfen* verwenden.	I have been able to carry these bags. They haven't been allowed to go to the cinema.

3.4 Das *present perfect*

Die Verwendung des *present perfect*

Signalwörter zeigen dir oft an, wann du das *present perfect* einsetzen musst.

Eine Handlung oder ein Ereignis ist gerade eben abgeschlossen worden: *just – gerade eben*

Simon has **just** listened to his new CD.
I have **just** finished my homework.

Eine Handlung oder ein Ereignis begann in der Vergangenheit und dauert bis in die Gegenwart an: *since / for – seit*

Anna has lived here **for** ten years.
She has lived here **since** 1999.

Eine Handlung oder ein Ereignis fand in der Vergangenheit statt, aber die Zeit wird nicht genau angegeben. Die Handlung selbst ist wichtig, nicht der Zeitpunkt: *already – schon* *not ... yet – noch nicht*

I have **already** seen the film.
I have**n't** been to the new shopping centre **yet**.

Die **Signalwörter** für das *present perfect* haben eine feste Stellung im Satz:
■ Unmittelbar **vor** dem *past participle* stehen:
never – niemals   *ever – jemals*
already – schon   *always – immer*
just – gerade eben   *often – oft*

Victoria has **already** packed.
He has **always** liked hamburgers.
I have **just** written a letter.

■ Immer am **Satzende** stehen:
before – vorher   *(not ...) yet – noch nicht*
so far – bisher

Victor has not packed **yet**.
Have you been to Scotland **before**?

■ **Vor der Zeitangabe** stehen:
since / for – seit

Margret has worked here **for** five months.
I have not seen my uncle **since** May.

Die **Verneinung** wird mit *not* gebildet, das immer nach *have / has* steht.

Have you seen my glasses? – No, I have not / haven't seen them.

Zur Bildung von **Fragen** im *present perfect*: ↑ Kap. 6.2!

Have you had lunch already?

45

Vergangenheit

 ÜBUNG 16 Hier sind verschiedene Verbformen durcheinandergeraten: Grundform, *simple past* und *past participle*. Unterstreiche alle Formen, die *past participle* sein können:

eaten – drink – thought – shown – sang – spoke – driven – eat – gone – done –

break – have – knew – were – write – written – fall – keep – know – drunk –

slept – show – ring – rung – begin – begun – been – was – stolen – became –

laugh – rang – taken – met

 ÜBUNG 17 Bilde die passende *present perfect*-Form: Trage sie in das Wortgitter ein und löse das Buchstabenrätsel.

1. to stop / he
2. to watch / we
3. to try / you
4. to laugh / he
5. to cycle / he
6. to allow / she
7. to look / she
8. to close / we
9. to pull / he
10. to live / I
11. to wash / she
12. to worry / they
13. to love / we
14. to dance / he

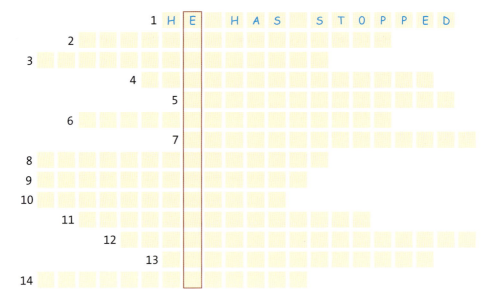

1 HE HAS STOPPED

with the dogs.

46

3.4 Das *present perfect*

ÜBUNG 18 Höre dir Track 5 auf der CD an und setze das *present perfect* ein.

Ida's bike is shining. She _____ just _____ it.

_____ you _____ your homework? – Yes, I _____ already _____ it.

Jim _____ take his medicine.

Look here, my hands are clean. I _____ just _____ them.

We have English at school. I _____ it for two years.

Marc _____ in Berlin for three years now.

We _____ to France yet.

Jane and Tim _____ the magazines. They don't need them anymore.

ÜBUNG 19 Trage die Übersetzung der Signalwörter für das *present perfect* in das Gitter ein.

1. seit (Zeitpunkt)
2. niemals
3. schon
4. seit (Zeitraum)
5. jemals
6. noch nicht

ÜBUNG 20 Signalwörter zeigen dir, dass das *present perfect* verwendet werden muss. Achte auf die Satzstellung und bilde einen passenden Satz! Schreibe die Lösungen in dein Übungsheft.

just: Gina / to write / a letter
never: I / to listen / to Indian music
for: Harry and Kim / to work / in a restaurant / nine months
already: we / can *(können)* book our trip / to Paris *(Ersatzform verwenden)*
not yet: He / can *(dürfen)* go / to London *(Ersatzform verwenden)*

47

Vergangenheit

 ÜBUNG 21 Übersetze und schreibe in dein Übungsheft.

Sie haben gerade ihre Arbeit beendet.
Sie hat gerade die Fenster geputzt.
Rosa lebt seit zwei Jahren in Rom *(Rome)*.
Ich habe die CD schon angehört.

WISSEN

Since und for im *present perfect*
Since und *for* sind eindeutige Signalwörter für das *present perfect*. Sie zeigen an, dass etwas in der Vergangenheit begonnen hat und in der Gegenwart noch andauert.

Achtung: Im Deutschen wird häufig das Präsens verwendet: I **have lived** in England for eight years. → Ich **lebe** seit acht Jahren in England.

since → **Zeitpunkt:**
Since zeigt an, wann eine Handlung oder ein Ereignis angefangen hat: since Monday, since 1947, since 8 o'clock.

for → **Zeitraum:**
For zeigt an, wie lange eine Handlung oder ein Ereignis bereits andauert: for two weeks, for six years, for a long time

 ÜBUNG 22 Zeitpunkt oder Zeitraum? Ordne die Zeitangaben der richtigen Spalte zu und schreibe jeweils *since* oder *for* dazu.

> two years – yesterday – one hour – 1984 – last October – ten months – the last two weeks – 9 o'clock – Friday – January 1st – Christmas – a long time – six days – one minute

since **(Zeitpunkt)**   *for* **(Zeitraum)**

3.4 Das *present perfect*

ÜBUNG 23 Die folgenden Sätze beschreiben, was einige Personen gerade tun *(present progressive)*. Setze die Handlungen ins *present perfect*. Schreibe in dein Übungsheft.

Beispiel: They are taking the dog for a walk. → They have taken the dog for a walk.

She is writing a birthday card.
He is making his bed.
I am doing my homework.
The dogs are eating the cake.

Michael is listening to the new CD.
My friends are buying a present.
Grandmother is reading the newspaper.

ÜBUNG 24 Formuliere ganze Sätze mithilfe der Stichwörter.

1. Frank looks unhappy (to lose, mobile phone).

   He has lost his mobile phone.

2. David and Peter are very tired (to walk, all the way home).

3. Ralph has got chocolate around his mouth (to eat, chocolate cake).

4. The car is damaged (Ruth, to have, accident).

5. Eric doesn't talk to me (I, to forget, birthday).

Vergangenheit

 ÜBUNG 25 Bilde Sätze im *present perfect* und entscheide, ob du *since* oder *for* benötigst. Schreibe die Sätze in dein Übungsheft.

I / to eat / Chinese food / I was 10 years old
Julia and Ron / to know / each other / 2007
the girls / to talk / on the phone / three hours

 ÜBUNG 26 Höre dir Track 6 auf der CD an und setze in die Lücken die richtige Form des *present perfect* ein.

The Greens and the Sanders are planning to go to the adventure park.

It's 8 o'clock in the morning.

Gina Green: "Mum, Dad, wake up! We _____ .
I _____ the alarm clock. Lisa _____
just _____ . The Sanders _____ already
_____ ."

(later)

Dad: "I _____ the picnic. _____ you
_____ a shower, Gina?"

Gina: "Yes, I _____ just _____ in the bathroom.
It's your turn now. _____ you _____
some biscuits and a bottle of water?"

Dad: "Yes, I _____ everything in the bag. But I
_____ our swimsuits."

Mum: "I _____ just _____ them on the table over there.

Gina: "Listen, the phone is ringing! ... *(a moment later)* Lisa _____
again. The Sanders _____ back home because they
_____ their money."

 ÜBUNG 27 Übersetze die folgenden Sätze. Schreibe sie in dein Übungsheft.

Ich habe das Buch schon gelesen.
Meine Mutter hat gerade eben angerufen.
Kate spielt seit vier Jahren Golf.
Richard hat schon Blumen gekauft.

3.5 Zeitformen der Vergangenheit im Vergleich

Wie im Deutschen gibt es im Englischen mehrere Zeitformen für die Vergangenheit:

▪ Ist eine Handlung in der Vergangenheit abgeschlossen, steht das *simple past*.

Yesterday I went for a walk.

▪ Wird der Handlungsablauf in der Vergangenheit betont, verwendest du das *past progressive*.

He was working all day long.

▪ Hat die Handlung eine Nachwirkung bis in die Gegenwart, benutze das *present perfect*.

Karen has learned English since April.

Simple past und *past progressive*

Wird der **Zeitpunkt** (→ *simple past)* oder der **Zeitraum** (→ *past progressive)* betont?

Warren wrote a letter yesterday.
Victoria was singing the whole day.

Begann eine Handlung vor einer anderen? → Die bereits andauernde Handlung steht im *past progressive*, die neu einsetzende Handlung im *simple past*.

We were having a party when my mother came home.
While Lisa was cooking, Aunt Helen arrived.

Simple past und *present perfect*

Ist die Handlung in der Vergangenheit komplett **abgeschlossen** und hat jetzt in der Gegenwart keine Bedeutung mehr, steht das *simple past*.

I did my homework on Monday.
She was unhappy yesterday.

Begann die Handlung in der Vergangenheit und **dauert bis jetzt an** oder hat jetzt noch einen Bezug zur Gegenwart, so muss das *present perfect* stehen. Abgeschlossene Handlung → *simple past*, Gegenwartsbezug → *present perfect*.

Sabrina has lived here for two months.
Tom has just finished the book.

Aufgepasst: Im Deutschen kann man verschiedene Vergangenheitsformen für die gleiche Situation verwenden, im Englischen nicht.

Gestern habe ich neue CDs gekauft. = Gestern kaufte ich neue CDs.
aber nur: I **bought** some CDs **yesterday.**

Vergangenheit

Wichtige unregelmäßige Verben *(irregular verbs)*

infinitive	*simple past*	*past participle*	*deutsche Bedeutung*
to be	was / were	been	sein
to begin	began	begun	anfangen
to break	broke	broken	zerbrechen
to buy	bought	bought	kaufen
to catch	caught	caught	fangen
to come	came	come	kommen
to do	did	done	machen, tun
to drink	drank	drunk	trinken
to drive	drove	driven	(Auto) fahren
to eat	ate	eaten	essen
to fall	fell	fallen	fallen
to find	found	found	finden
to forget	forgot	forgotten	vergessen
to get	got	got	bekommen
to give	gave	given	geben
to go	went	gone	gehen
to have	had	had	haben
to hear	heard	heard	hören
to know	knew	known	kennen, wissen
to leave	left	left	verlassen
to lose	lost	lost	verlieren
to make	made	made	machen
to meet	met	met	treffen
to pay	paid	paid	bezahlen
to run	ran	run	laufen
to say	said	said	sagen
to see	saw	seen	sehen
to sell	sold	sold	verkaufen
to send	sent	sent	schicken
to show	showed	shown	zeigen
to stand	stood	stood	stehen
to take	took	taken	nehmen
to teach	taught	taught	unterrichten
to tell	told	told	erzählen
to think	thought	thought	denken
to win	won	won	gewinnen
to write	wrote	written	schreiben

3.5 Zeitformen der Vergangenheit im Vergleich

ÜBUNG 28 Im Wortspeicher ist alles durcheinandergeraten: *simple past-*, *past progressive-* und *present perfect*-Formen. Ordne richtig in die Tabelle ein.

> threw – have drawn – was eating – went – were going – has gone – were doing – listened – was cleaning – has bought – have seen – visited – lost – has slept – did – was wearing – have told – were having

simple past	past progressive	present perfect

ÜBUNG 29 Hier hast du einige rätselhafte Sätze. Trage die Vergangenheitsform als Überschrift ein und bilde aus den durcheinandergeratenen Buchstaben die richtige Verbform. Schreibe die richtigen Sätze in dein Übungsheft. Ein Tipp: Die Grundformen der Verben stehen am Ende der Sätze.

1. _____

   Gina GCAWWTHISAN TV and Andrew TASTWINGIS next to her. (to watch, to sit).
   While they IRGEEALKWWN home, a bus passed them. (to walk)

2. _____

   At 8 o'clock I TEA some bread, RKAND a cup of tea and OKOT the bus. (to eat, to drink, to take)

3. _____

   Uncle John TAWRHTESIN six postcards since he left. (to write)
   I HEVA just TEDRUN off the radio. (to turn)

53

Vergangenheit

ÜBUNG 30 Die Wörterschlange hat immer die gleiche Reihenfolge: *infinitive – simple past – present perfect – infinitive – simple past* usw. Fülle die Lücken richtig aus.

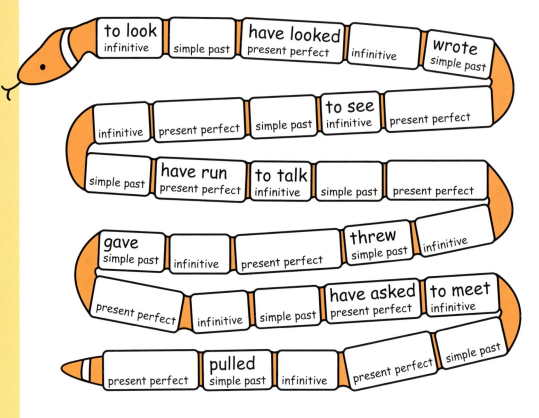

ÜBUNG 31 Nun musst du dich entscheiden: *simple past* oder *present perfect*? Achte auf die Signalwörter.

Last Christmas we _____ (to have) turkey (*Truthahn*) for dinner.

Sarah _____ (to write) the e-mail two weeks ago.

Grandma _____ just _____ (to arrive).

Max and Tina _____ (to go) to England last year.

Dana _____ (to be) to England _____ (since / for) three months.

Mum _____ (to wear) her new dress last Sunday.

Victor _____ never _____ (to wear) his new jeans so far.

The Millers _____ (to paint) their house in March. It is pink and yellow now.

54

3.5 Zeitformen der Vergangenheit im Vergleich

ÜBUNG 32 Setze *simple past, past progressive* oder *present perfect* ein. Achte auf alle Signalwörter und den Zeitraum oder Zeitpunkt der Handlung!

1. Yesterday Gina _____ (to eat) pizza for dinner.

   Rachel _____ (to eat) pizza for the last three days.

   I _____ (to eat) pizza when Eddy _____ (to come) along.

2. While Emma _____ (to walk) to school, she _____ (to meet) Sam.

   I _____ (to walk) home yesterday.

   She _____ just _____ (to walk) through the door.

3. He _____ just _____ (to write) the letter.

   I _____ (to write) a postcard when the phone _____ (to ring).

   They _____ (to write) an e-mail two weeks ago.

ÜBUNG 33 Bilde einen Satz mit einer Hintergrundhandlung und einem plötzlich einsetzenden Ereignis. Verwende immer abwechselnd beim ersten Satz *when*, beim zweiten Satz *while*. Schreibe in dein Übungsheft.

Hintergrundhandlung	plötzlich einsetzendes Ereignis
Fred – to have breakfast	suddenly – the fire alarm – to start

Fred was having breakfast when suddenly the fire alarm started.

we – to sit in the park	a dog – to jump – at us

While ...

they – to work in the garden	a mouse – to run – through the bushes
Joan – to sell clothes in a shop	someone – to steal – a shirt
I – to ride my bike – in the forest	a rabbit – to cross – my path
they – to take pictures	the battery – to die
Liz – to watch a film	someone – to scream
Sally – to read the newspapers	suddenly – her Dad's name – to discover

55

Vergangenheit

Klassenarbeit 1

 45 Minuten

 AUFGABE 1 Handelt es sich bei den folgenden Sätzen um *simple past*, *past progressive* oder *present perfect*? Kreuze an. Unterstreiche das Signalwort.

	simple past	past progressive	present perfect
Father has just arrived here.	☐	☐	☐
Verena bought a new board two weeks ago.	☐	☐	☐
I have learned English for two years.	☐	☐	☐
While the baby was playing, its mother ...	☐	☐	☐
Have you ever seen a Shakespeare play?	☐	☐	☐
We walked all the way to the city centre on Monday.	☐	☐	☐
Tony has played the piano for one hour.	☐	☐	☐

AUFGABE 2 Ergänze die fehlenden Formen.

Grundform	simple past	past participle
to run		
	bought	
		been
to think		
		written
	knew	
to leave		
to speak		
		told
to meet		
	stood	
to win		
		gotten
	gave	
		done

56

Klassenarbeiten

AUFGABE 3 Entscheide dich – setze *simple past* oder *past progressive* ein.

While Lena _____ (to sleep), the dog suddenly _____ (to bark).

Rosa _____ (to sit) at the lake when someone _____ (to scream).

While Mrs Turner _____ (to wait) for the bus and Tina _____ (to talk) to her best friend, an accident _____ (to happen).

They _____ (to eat) ice cream when the thief _____ (to take) the bag.

I _____ (to read) a book and my brother _____ (to study), when mum came home.

The boys _____ (to play) cards when the bell _____ (to ring).

AUFGABE 4 Signalwörter zeigen dir, welche Zeitform du verwenden musst. Ordne sie der richtigen Zeitform in der Tabelle zu.

> yesterday – so far – last week – since last July – one week ago – for two days – never – in 1983 – last year – just – already – last summer

Signalwörter für *simple past*	Signalwörter für *present perfect*

Vergangenheit

AUFGABE 5 Formuliere kurze Merksätze. Wann verwendet man *simple past*, *past progressive* oder *present perfect?* Nenne Signalwörter.

past progressive:
Das *past progressive* wird verwendet, um den ▭ einer Handlung
zu betonen.
Signalwörter sind: w ▭ , w ▭

simple past:
Das *simple past* wird verwendet, wenn eine Handlung in der
▭ abgeschlossen ist.
Signalwörter sind: y ▭ , l ▭ y ▭ , one w ▭ a ▭

present perfect:
Das *present perfect* wird verwendet, wenn eine Handlung in der
▭ begonnen hat und in der ▭
noch von Bedeutung ist.
Signalwörter sind: s ▭ , f ▭ , j ▭ , alr ▭ , y ▭

AUFGABE 6 Setze die fehlende Zeitform ein. Entscheide dich zwischen *simple past*, *past progressive* oder *present perfect*.

Susan and Lisa ▭ (to ride) their bikes when the rain

▭ (to start).

Benny ▭ (to learn) three languages ▭ (since / for) 2001.

My friends ▭ just ▭ (to arrive) at the restaurant.

Leonardo da Vinci ▭ (to paint) the Mona Lisa in 1503.

The girls ▭ (to talk) to each other while the boys

▭ (to play) with the dogs.

I ▭ (to buy) the tomatoes three days ago.

The family ▭ (to live) in America ▭ (since / for)

ten years now.

Mrs George ▭ already ▭ (to read) three books

by John Steinbeck.

58

Klassenarbeiten

Klassenarbeit 2

 60 Minuten

AUFGABE 7 Nenne, zu welcher englischen Zeit die folgenden Verbformen gehören.

was / were + ing-Form des Verbs →

am / are / is + ing-Form des Verbs →

personal pronoun + past (simple) form →

had been + ing-Form des Verbs →

AUFGABE 8 Setze die angegeben Verben in die richtige Form.

he / to drink / simple past →

they / to see / past progressive →

we / to have / simple past →

she / to read / present progressive →

I / to watch / simple past →

you / to leave / past progressive →

AUFGABE 9 *Present perfect simple.* Schreibe vollständige Sätze.

Mary / to finish / her homework

Mr Miller / to wash / his car

Lilly / to write / a letter

The guests / to eat / a delicious meal

Grandma / to bake / a cake

Vergangenheit

 AUFGABE 10 *Present perfect* oder *simple past*? Schreibe zuerst eine Frage, dann die passende Antwort in dein Übungsheft.

Beispiel: to be to Hollywood / yes / to go there in 2009 → Have you ever been to Hollywood? Yes, I have. I went there in 2009.

ever / to swim in the Atlantic Ocean / yes / last year
ever / to play beach volleyball / no
ever / to go skiing / yes / last Christmas
ever / to ride a mountainbike / yes / last summer in Switzerland
ever / to drink champagne / yes / on my 14th birthday
ever / to lose a pair of shoes / yes / last summer

 AUFGABE 11 *Mixed tenses*. Schreibe die richtigen Formen in die Lücken. Achte auf die korrekte Zeit.

Mother came in to Mia's room while she _____ (to cry).

What are you doing at the moment? – I _____ (to wash) the dishes.

While Laura _____ (to wait) for her school bus, she _____ (to see) an accident happen.

When Hannah _____ (to be) a little girl, her family _____ (to live) in New Zealand.

The sun _____ (to rise) every morning.

Lilly always _____ (to finish) her homework before she meets her friends.

Mother _____ (to visit) grandmother in hospital twice since last Friday.

Two years ago, while John _____ (to travel) through Australia, an earthquake happened.

 AUFGABE 12 Übersetze. Schreibe in dein Übungsheft.

Meine Schwester lebt seit zwei Jahren in Irland.
War Laura gestern auf Peters Party?
Mary spielt seit fünf Jahren Klavier.
Wer hat dir denn diese Geschichte erzählt?
Ich bin gestern ins Kino gegangen und habe Eis gegessen.

Klassenarbeit 3

Klassenarbeiten

60 Minuten

AUFGABE 13 Gib vom jeweiligen Verb die angegebene Form an.

to keep / *simple present* →

to forget / *past participle* →

to put / *past participle* →

to ride / *simple past* →

to ride / *past participle* →

to buy / *simple past* →

to eat / *simple past* →

to do / *past participle* →

AUFGABE 14 Sarah erzählt von ihrem letzten Campingurlaub. Setze das angegebene Verb in die richtige Form.

A year ago my friends and I _____ (to take) the train to Scotland.

We _____ (to go) with other children from our youth club.

Tessa and I _____ (to organise) the holiday. Our club leader

_____ (to help), of course. We _____ (to stay) in tents.

We _____ (to cook) our own meals. We _____ (to walk)

to a lot of interesting places there. We _____ (to have) a lot of fun.

I really _____ (to like) last year's holidays!

AUFGABE 15 *Simple past* oder *past progressive*?

When Peter's mother _____ (to come) into Peter's room she

_____ (to see) that he and his friends _____ (to play)

a computer game. She _____ (to tell) them to stop. Peter, however,

_____ (to tell) his mother that they _____ (to play) a

harmless game and _____ (to ask) his mother to leave his room.

Peter's mother _____ (to get) very angry. She _____

(to leave) the room, but _____ (to give) her son a fierce glance.

Vergangenheit

 AUFGABE 16 Formuliere Fragen. Frage nach den unterstrichenen Satzgliedern. Schreibe in dein Übungsheft.

Mary read a book last night.
Last summer, Lisa travelled to Spain.
Sarah took Jamie's book.
Somebody stole my bike.
Last Friday night, I stayed at home because I had a fever.
I want to speak to Mary.
Megan saw a dead rat.

 AUFGABE 17 Formuliere ganze Sätze. Verwende immer das *past progressive*.

Last Saturday, ...

the dog / to chase / the cat

Mr Miller / to wash / the dishes

the children / to watch / TV

the sun / to shine

... when the telephone rang and Mrs Miller's sister called from New Zealand.

 AUFGABE 18 Formuliere zu den Sätzen aus Aufgabe 17 passende Fragen. Schreibe in dein Übungsheft.

 AUFGABE 19 *Simple past* oder *past progressive*? Schreibe vollständige Sätze in dein Übungsheft.

While the Millers / to watch TV / a burglar / to break into / their garage.
Grandma Elisabeth / to clean / the kitchen window / to see / an accident. She / to go / to the phone / to call / the police.
Maggie / to do her homework / when / to hear / a strange noise. She / to look outside / and / see / the hail *(Hagel)*.

4

Zukunft

4.1 Das *will-future*

Die Bildung des *will-future*

Im Englischen gibt es mehrere Möglichkeiten, die Zukunft auszudrücken, unter anderem das *will-future* und das *going to-future*.

Das *will-future* wird mit **will** und dem **Infinitiv** (ohne *to*) gebildet.

Aussage:
will + Infinitiv (ohne *to*)

Anna will marry one day.

Verneinung:
will + *not* + Infinitiv (ohne *to*)
(Kurzform: *won't*)

Anna will not / won't marry one day.

Frage:
will-Form vor das *Subjekt* stellen

Will Anna marry one day?

Die Verwendung des *will-future*

Das *will future* wird verwendet bei
■ unbeeinflussbaren Ereignissen und Zuständen in der Zukunft,

■ Vermutungen, Hoffnungen und Voraussagen,

■ spontanen Entscheidungen für die nahe Zukunft,

■ Bedingungssätzen mit *if* (↑ Kap. 5.3).

It will be warm tomorrow. (→ Das Wetter kann niemand beeinflussen.)
It will be Sarah's birthday next Monday. (→ Daran kann niemand etwas ändern.)
I think she will call me. (→ Du vermutest, dass sie anrufen wird.)
I hope we will have fun. (→ Du hoffst, dass ihr eine lustige Zeit miteinander verbringen werdet.)
You look hungry. I will make you a sandwich. (→ Du fällst eine spontane Entscheidung.)
If you run, you will reach the bus. (→ Bedingung: Du musst rennen; Folge: Du wirst den Bus erreichen.)

WISSEN

Zukunft

ÜBUNG 1 Höre dir Track 7 auf der CD an und setze das *will-future* ein.

1. **Unbeeinflussbare Ereignisse und Zustände in der Zukunft**

    We have tickets for the cinema. We _____ you later.

    We must go now or we _____ the bus.

2. **Vermutungen, Hoffnungen und Voraussagen**

    Don't eat so much chocolate. You _____ fat.

    I think Manchester United _____ the football match.

3. **Spontane Entscheidungen für die nahe Zukunft**

    Do you need sugar? Wait, I _____ some.

    You look unhappy. I _____ .

4. **Verwendung in Bedingungssätzen mit *if***

    If I get a mountain bike, we _____ on a cycling holiday.

    If I don't find the way, I _____ a policeman.

ÜBUNG 2 Formuliere selbst Sätze zu den vier Verwendungsmöglichkeiten des *will-future* (siehe Übung 1). Beachte die Satzstellung Subjekt – Verb – Objekt und schreibe in dein Übungsheft.

1. It's snowing. – a traffic jam / in the evening / to be / there
2. Tomorrow there's a party at Lisa's. – come / to the party / John / too
3. Stop! There is an accident. – to call / I / the police
4. If the weather is bad, – not / to play / we / in the garden

WISSEN

Die Kurzform des *will-future*
Du hast bisher hauptsächlich die **Langform** des *will-future* (will/will not) kennengelernt. Häufig wird auch die **Kurzform** benutzt. Die Kurzform wird eher beim Sprechen verwendet, die Langform meist beim Schreiben.

will + Infinitiv (ohne *to*) → 'll
Wait, I'll get some sugar.
We'll see you tomorrow.

will + *not* + Infinitiv (ohne *to*) → won't
I won't go.
We won't ask him.

4.1 Das *will-future*

ÜBUNG 3 Setze die fehlende *will*-Form (Langform) ein und kreuze an, welche der vier Verwendungsmöglichkeiten (siehe Übung 1) vorliegt.

	(1)	(2)	(3)	(4)
Okay, we _____ (to do) it right now.	☐	☐	☐	☐
I'm ill. I hope my friend _____ (to visit) me.	☐	☐	☐	☐
If I meet them, I _____ (to tell) them.	☐	☐	☐	☐
Don't worry, we _____ (to help) you.	☐	☐	☐	☐
Tomorrow the weather _____ (to be) fine.	☐	☐	☐	☐
I'm sure Tim _____ (not/to be) angry.	☐	☐	☐	☐

WISSEN

Signalwörter helfen
Vermutungen und Hoffnungen, bei denen das *will-future* verwendet wird, sind oft gekennzeichnet durch **Signalwörter** wie:

I think – ich glaube   *I hope* – ich hoffe   *perhaps* – vielleicht
I suppose – ich vermute   *I am sure* – ich bin sicher *probably* – wahrscheinlich

ÜBUNG 4 Wie wirst du in 25 Jahren leben? Formuliere Hoffnungen und Voraussagen über dein zukünftiges Leben, indem du die Stichwörter benutzt.

Beispiel: hope: rich / happy → I hope I will be rich and happy.

think: travel / around the world
sure: live / big house
suppose: look / like / film star
perhaps: president / Germany

ÜBUNG 5 Übersetze. Schreibe die Sätze in dein Übungsheft.

Wir glauben, Phil kommt morgen.
Wird es nicht regnen?
Morgen wirst du vielleicht meinen Freund sehen.
Falls das Geschäft öffnet, werden wir einkaufen.
Ich werde nicht zu Simons Party gehen.

4.2 Das *going to-future*

Die Bildung des *going to-future*

Auch mit dem *going to-future* kann man ein zukünftiges Ereignis ausdrücken. Es wird mit einer Form von **to be** und **going to** und dem **Infinitiv** (ohne *to*) gebildet.

Aussage:
to be + *going to* + Infinitiv (ohne *to*)

We are going to have a party on Saturday.

Verneinung:
to be + *not going to* + Infinitiv (ohne *to*)

They are not going to come to our party.

Frage:
Hilfsverb *to be* vor das Subjekt stellen

Are you going to wear a shirt for the party?

Für die Bildung des *going to-future* brauchst du die Formen von **to be**.

Singular: I am, you are, he / she / it is

Plural: we are, you are, they are

Aufgepasst: Verwechsle nicht die Verlaufsform der Gegenwart (*present progressive*) mit dem *going to-future*!

I'm going home (Verlaufsform).
→ Ich gehe gerade nach Hause.

Aber: I'm going to go home (*going to-future*)
→ Ich werde nach Hause gehen.

Die Verwendung des *going to-future*

Das *going to-future* wird verwendet bei:
- festen Vorhaben, Verabredungen, Plänen und bereits gefällten Entscheidungen,

I am going to visit my friend at the weekend. (→ Du hast das fest vor.)

These are the ingredients (*Zutaten*). I am going to make a cake. (→ Dein Entschluss steht fest.)

- Voraussagen, die mit großer Sicherheit eintreten werden oder absehbar sind.

Tom is going to do his homework this afternoon. (→ Wenn nichts dazwischen kommt, wird er seine Hausaufgaben erledigen.)

Look, the ladder is broken. Liz is going to fall down. (→ Es ist absehbar, dass Liz herunterfällt, da die Leiter kaputt ist.)

4.2 Das *going to-future*

4

ÜBUNG 6   Setze die richtigen Formen des *going to-future* ein.

1. **Feste Vorhaben, Verabredungen, Pläne, gefällte Entscheidungen**

   David _____ (to meet) his father after school.

   I _____ (to stay) at home next weekend.

   Dad _____ (to do) the washing-up after lunch.

   Our teacher promised: we _____ (listen) to pop songs.

2. **Mit großer Sicherheit eintretende oder absehbare Voraussagen**

   Look at the clouds. It _____ (to rain).

   Ann has got a cloth *(Tuch)* in her hand. She _____

   (to clean) her bike.

   Aunt Helen called. Sue and Kim _____ (to visit) her

   tomorrow.

ÜBUNG 7   Setze die fehlende *going to*-Zukunftsform ein und kreuze an, welche der
zwei Anwendungsmöglichkeiten (siehe Übung 6) vorliegt.

	(1)	(2)
Jim has got toothache. He _____ (to see) the dentist.	☐	☐
Look here. I _____ (to eat) your cookie.	☐	☐
We _____ (to move) to Italy next year.	☐	☐
Look at the ship. It _____ (to sink).	☐	☐
My plans for Saturday: I _____ (to do) a lot of sports.	☐	☐
Jane _____ (not / to come).	☐	☐

She had an accident yesterday.

ÜBUNG 8   Will, Sandra, Dave und Betty haben verschiedene Pläne für das Wochenende.
Formuliere Sätze mit dem *going to-future*. Schreibe in dein Übungsheft.

Beispiel: Ralph is going to clean his bike on Sunday at 7 p.m.

Will	Sandra	Dave	Betty	you
Saturday	Sunday	Saturday	Sunday	Saturday
4 p.m.	9 a.m.	2 p.m.	3 p.m.	11 a.m.
play football	go to the lake	visit Francis	watch Formula 1	?

ÜBEN

67

Zukunft

WISSEN

Die Kurzform des *going to*-future
Beim *going to-future (am / is / are going to)* gibt es wie beim *will-future* eine **Langform** und eine **Kurzform**. Die Kurzform wird eher beim Sprechen verwendet, die Langform meist beim Schreiben.

am → 'm	I'm going to eat the cake.
is → 's	He's going to play in the garden.
are → 're	We're going to meet Jill at the station.
am not → 'm not	I'm not going to work here.
is not → 's not / isn't	She's not / isn't going to do her homework.
are not → 're not / aren't	They're not / aren't going to ask him.

 ÜBUNG 9 Setze die fehlenden *going to*-Formen ein.

Pat: "Look at those clouds. It _____ (to rain) soon."

Kim: "Don't worry. We _____ (to reach, *erreichen*) the next village in five minutes. So we _____ (not / to get) wet."

Pat: "That's not right. The next village is three miles away. And look, the first raindrops! We _____ (to get) wet."

Kim: "What _____ (we / to do) now?"

Pat: "Look, there's a shelter *(Unterstand)*. We _____ (to wait) there until the rain stops."

 ÜBUNG 10 Übersetze die Sätze ins Englische und schreibe sie in dein Übungsheft. Überlege dir, ob es sich um ein festes Vorhaben (1) oder eine absehbare Voraussage (2) handelt und schreibe die Zahlen dazu.

Schau mal, das kleine Mädchen! Sie wird gleich vom Fahrrad fallen *(to fall off)*.
Wirst du deine Ferien in Italien verbringen?
Schau dir die Wolken an! Es wird schneien.
Hier sind die Karten *(tickets)*. Wir werden am Samstag zu dem Open-Air-Konzert gehen.

4.3 *Will-future* und *going to-future* im Vergleich

Will-future:
- unbeeinflussbare Ereignisse
- Vermutungen, Hoffnungen, Voraussagen
- spontane Entscheidungen
→ **wahrscheinlich eintretende Zukunft**

It will be warm and sunny.
I hope she will not be angry.

I will help you.

Going to-future:
- feste Vorhaben, Verabredungen, Pläne und bereits gefällte Entscheidungen
- Voraussagen, die mit großer Sicherheit eintreten werden oder absehbar sind
→ **fest geplante Zukunft**

He is going to play volleyball on Monday.
We are going to see grandma tomorrow.
I am not going to pass the exams.
Dean is going to win the match on Sunday.

Besonderheiten

Die **Hilfsverben** *can, may* und *must* dürfen **nicht** mit *will* oder *going to* kombiniert werden!

Benutze stattdessen die Ersatzformen *be able to, be allowed to* und *have to* (↑ Kap. 2.2 und 2.3).

I will be able to drive a car when I'm 18.
I hope I will be allowed to go outside.
I will have to go home.

Aufgepasst: Mit *will* wird eine zukünftige Handlung ausgedrückt. Beim deutschen *wollen* musst du *want to* verwenden.

I will go *(will-future)*. → Ich werde gehen.
I want to go *(simple present)*. – Ich *will* gehen.

Merke: Bei **Fragen** und **Verneinungen** steht niemals *to do*, da bereits ein Hilfsverb vorhanden ist: *will* beim *will-future*, *to be* beim *going to-future*.

Will the weather be nice tomorrow?
Are you going to meet Jean on Monday?
I hope she will not come.
He is not going to come.

WISSEN

Zukunft

ÜBUNG 11 Wann verwendet man das *will-future* und wann das *going to-future*? Schließe das Buch, schreibe die Verwendungsformen auf ein leeres Blatt und vergleiche deine Antwort dann mit der vorherigen Seite.

ÜBUNG 12 Kennzeichne die Sätze, die das *will-future* benötigen, mit *w* und die Aussagen, bei denen das *going to-future* stehen muss, mit *g*.

Ereignisse, die du nicht beeinflussen kannst:

Du hoffst, dass etwas eintritt:

Ihr habt einen festen Plan für das kommende Wochenende:

Du entscheidest dich ganz spontan, deinem Freund zu helfen:

Du beobachtest zwei Autos, die gleich zusammenstoßen werden:

Wenn du Arzt bist *(Bedingung!)*, dann wirst du Leben retten:

ÜBUNG 13 Spontane Entscheidung *(will-future)* oder fester Vorsatz *(going to-future)*? Setze die passende Zukunftsform ein.

Randy: "Look here, my bike. I can't use it, the brakes *(Bremsen)* are not working.

My dad _____ (to repair) it on Saturday."

Simon: "Don't wait until Saturday. I _____ (to check) it for you."

Randy: "Thanks a lot. But I need new brakes. Dad and I

_____ (to buy) them on Saturday. Do you want to

come with us?"

Simon: "Yes, of course, I _____ (to come), too."

4.3 *Will-future* und *going to-future* im Vergleich

ÜBUNG 14 Formuliere Fragen in der passenden Zukunftsform.

_____ (you / to watch) the match on Sunday? – No, I'm not.

_____ (Ralph / to like) my dog? – No, he won't. He hates dogs.

_____ (sun / to shine) tomorrow? – Yes, it will.

_____ (what / you / to do) on Tuesday? – I'm not sure yet.

ÜBUNG 15 Ruth ist bei einer Wahrsagerin (*fortune teller*). Füge die passende Zukunftsform ein. Überlege genau, ob es sich um eine Vorhersage (*will-future*) oder ein festes Vorhaben (*going to-future*) handelt.

Fortune teller: "You _____ (to be) happy all your life."

Ruth: "That's nice. I _____ (to have) a party next Sunday. _____ (it / to be) a good party?"

Fortune teller: "Let's see. Yes, it _____ (to be) good. And a nice boy _____ (to come) to the party. His name is Andrew."

Ruth: "Yes, you are right. Andrew _____ (to come). I invited him."

ÜBUNG 16 Setze entweder *will-future* oder *going to-future* in die Lücken ein.

What about next Friday? – I _____ (to play) basketball with my friends.

I've got a headache. – Have you? Wait here and I _____ (to get) a glass of water for you.

Why are you filling this bucket with water? – I _____ (to wash) the car.

If you take the dog for a walk, it _____ (to bark) anymore.

It's decided (*entschieden*), they _____ (to build) a new house. It _____ (to be) very noisy the next months.

71

Zukunft
Klassenarbeit 1

 45 Minuten

 AUFGABE 1 Unterstreiche die Zukunftsformen. Bezeichne die Art der zukünftigen Handlung.

She hopes he <u>will come back</u> this evening: will → Hoffnung

Look at him, I will help him with his heavy bags. →

Oh no, the dog is going to bite *(beißen)* her. →

We are going to buy a present for mum on Saturday. →

 AUFGABE 2 Hier geht es um unbeeinflussbare Ereignisse, Hoffnungen, Vermutungen und spontane Entscheidungen. Setze die passende Zukunftsform ein.

Ben: "I hope we _____ (not / to get) too much homework for today. What _____ (the weather / to be) like in the afternoon?"

Paul: "I think it _____ (to be) nice and sunny in the afternoon. If we do not get a lot of homework, we _____ (to have) time to play together."

Ben: "We can ask our teacher. I hope she _____ (not / to give) us too much homework."

 AUFGABE 3 Hier werden Verabredungen, Pläne und absehbare Ereignisse beschrieben. Setze die passende Zukunftsform ein.

Mary: "_____ (you / to come) to our party on Saturday? We _____ (to have) a barbecue *(Grillfest)*."

Sandra: "Yes, I _____ (to come). My mum _____ (to get) some veggie burgers."

Mary: "_____ (you / to sleep) here?"

Sandra: "No, my mum _____ (to pick) me up after the party."

Klassenarbeiten

AUFGABE 4 Setze *will-* oder *going to-future* ein.

If I go to Edinburgh, I _____ (to visit) my aunt.
_____ (you / to buy) a bike?
We _____ (to have) lasagne for dinner.
I think I _____ (to like) this work.

AUFGABE 5 Füge die Elemente zu Sätzen zusammen und entscheide dich für die richtige Zukunftsform. Schreibe in dein Übungsheft.

(Year 2030: You are a pilot) a pilot – to be – I
We hope – happy – she – to be – in Australia
to play football – on Sunday – you – ?
(You look tired:) not – we – to climb up – the hill
(Our plans for Saturday changed:) not – we – to climb up – the hill

AUFGABE 6 Übersetze die Frage und gib eine verneinte Antwort.

Wird sie den Test bestehen *(to pass)*?
_____
_____

Werde ich glücklich sein?
_____
_____

Wird Richard am Wochenende kommen?
_____
_____

Werdet ihr zusammen *(together)* spielen?
_____
_____

AUFGABE 7 Wie sieht deine Zukunft aus? Bilde zu den Stichwörtern Sätze mit der passenden Zukunftsform. Schreibe in dein Übungsheft.

Beispiel: Ein fester Plan für nächstes Jahr. → I'm going to learn a lot.

Ein fester Plan für nächsten Monat.
Eine Vorhersage über deinen zukünftigen Beruf.
Ein festes Vorhaben für nächste Woche.
Eine Vorhersage über das Wetter am nächsten Wochenende.
Eine Vorhersage über deinen zukünftigen Wohnort.

Zukunft

Klassenarbeit 2

 45 Minuten

 AUFGABE 8 Unterstreiche die richtige Verbform.

Look at the sky. It will snow / is going to snow any minute now.

I think it will rain / is going to rain tomorrow.

Sally can't go out tonight. She will do / is going to do her homework.

Are you going to the cinema? Wait a minute. I will go / am going to go with you.

My dad has made up his mind. He will stop / is going to stop smoking.

If you go by train next week, I will take / am going to take you to the station.

 AUFGABE 9 Was passiert als nächstes? Lies dir die folgenden Situationen durch und wähle dann das richtige Verb aus dem Wortspeicher, um zu beschreiben, was als Nächstes mit großer Wahrscheinlichkeit passieren wird. Verwende das *going to-future*.

> to fall down – to break – to walk into – to drop – to rain –
> to crash into – to write

Penny is carrying a lot of books that are too heavy for her. She _____ some of them.

There are lot of dark clouds in the sky. It _____ .

Jack isn't careful enough and there is a man standing right in front of him. He _____ that man.

Dave is in his classroom and he has got some chalk. He _____ something on the board.

Luke is driving far too quickly. Hopefully, he isn't _____ into a tree.

Look, there are two boys ice skating, but the temperatures are above zero. The ice _____ .

Mrs Snyder's cat has climbed up her tree again. It's Kitty again at the top of tree. She _____ . Poor thing. Last time the firemen had to rescue her.

74

Klassenarbeiten

AUFGABE 10 *Will-future* oder *going to-future*: Wähle die richtige Verbform.

Brian, I'm sure you _____ (to enjoy) your stay in

Wales. Maybe the weather _____ (to be) fantastic.

There are hardly any clouds. So the sun _____ (to shine).

We bought a house in York last year. We _____ (to move)

up north.

Do you think it _____ (to be) cold tomorrow?

Would you like to come to Angela's birthday party? – Well, I

_____ (to think) about it.

Perhaps Sue _____ (to meet) him again one day.

I'm afraid Matthew can't come tonight. He _____ (to play)

in an important football match tomorrow.

Kim _____ (to have) a proper breakfast before she

goes hiking.

AUFGABE 11 Korrigiere die folgenden Sätze und schreibe sie noch einmal
in der richtigen Zukunftsform in dein Übungsheft.

It is wet when we arrive in the Lake District.
Pete looks for a job in London.
Be careful. It is raining and there are a lot of leaves on the ground. You are slipping.
Will loves travelling. He travels for a year.
Jane's birthday is on a Wednesday this year.
Wait a minute! I'm helping you.
If I don't go to bed early, I'm tired the next day.
Look at this kitchen table: butter, sugar, flour. Mum will make a cake.

AUFGABE 12 Übersetze die folgenden Sätze ins Englische. Achte dabei auf die richtige
Verwendung der Zukunft. Schreibe in dein Übungsheft.

Ich bin nicht sicher, ob ich dieses Fahrrad kaufe.
Zoe hat Konzertkarten. Sie geht am Freitag ins Konzert.
Pam und Lucy haben fest vor, am Wochenende eine Party zu feiern.
Weihnachten ist dieses Jahr an einem Sonntag.
Setz dich. Ich schließe das Fenster.

Der Satz

5.1 Bejahte Aussagesätze

Präge dir die englische Satzstellung ein: **Subjekt + (Hilfsverb +) Vollverb + Ergänzungen**	My brother ↓ goes ↓ to primary school. ↓ We ↓ were ↓ drinking ↓ tea. ↓ Subjekt Hilfsverb Vollverb Ergänzungen
Das *simple present* und das *simple past* werden **ohne Hilfsverb** gebildet.	She lives in London. She learned English.
Mit Hilfsverb + Vollverb werden gebildet: ▪ *will-future: will* + Vollverb ▪ *going to-future: to be + going to* + Vollverb ▪ *past progressive: was / were* + Vollverb + *-ing*-Form ▪ *present perfect: to have + past participle* ▪ **Modalsätze:** Modalverb + Vollverb	He **will be** happy. They **are going to meet** Ann. Sally **was wearing** a funny dress. Lucy **has tidied** her room. We **must study** for the test. I **can sing** a song.
Aufgepasst: Die Satzstellung im Englischen unterscheidet sich vom Deutschen. ▪ Englisch: Subjekt + Hilfsverb + **Vollverb + Objekt** ▪ Deutsch: Subjekt + Hilfsverb + **Objekt + Vollverb**	I can repair the bike. *Aber:* Ich kann das Fahrrad reparieren. We must visit him. *Aber:* Wir müssen ihn besuchen.

Konjunktionen (Bindewörter)

Konjunktionen verbinden Wörter und Satzteile miteinander. Es gibt ▪ **einfache** Verbindungen: *and, or, but, because, so (daher), when (als), although (obwohl),* ▪ **gepaarte** Verbindungen: *either ... or (entweder ... oder), neither ... nor (weder noch).*	We sat down **because** we were tired. They were unhappy **so** they left. You can **either** go to Greece **or** to Spain. Tina **neither** likes oranges **nor** apples.

5.1 Bejahte Aussagesätze

ÜBUNG 1 Bilde aus Subjekt und Verb einen Satz. Achte auf die Zeitform und füge eine passende Satzergänzung aus dem Wortspeicher hinzu.

> a present – my clothes – the table – ~~a bottle of water~~ – a letter – the Prince of Wales – to the shop

simple past: Mrs Taylor – to drink

Mrs Taylor drank a bottle of water.

simple past: James – her – to give

simple present: can – he – write

past progressive: George and his brother – to go

present perfect: Richard – to paint

simple present: must – I – to change

going to-future: the Queen – to meet

WISSEN

Adverbialbestimmungen und Adverbien
Achte besonders auf die Stellung von Adverbialbestimmungen der Zeit, des Ortes sowie von Adverbien.
■ Im Deutschen steht die Zeitangabe vor der Ortsangabe, im Englischen ist es umgekehrt: **Ort vor Zeit!**
■ **Adverbien der Häufigkeit** wie *always, ever, never, often, sometimes* stehen in der Regel **vor** dem Vollverb.
■ **Adverbien der Art und Weise** stehen normalerweise hinter dem Objekt.

Ich war um 17 Uhr im Supermarkt.
Aber: I was at the supermarket at five.

Peter **sometimes** does the dishes.
I have **never** seen such a thing.

She answered the questions **nervously**.
She laughed **happily**.

77

Der Satz

ÜBUNG 2 Ordne die Satzteile zu ganzen Sätzen. Achte auf die Satzstellung.
Schreibe in dein Übungsheft.

simple present: I – to play CDs – often
simple past: in his room – he – sometimes – to listen to music – in the evenings
simple present: Tina – to visit – never – her grandmother
going to-future: on Sunday – my father – to play badminton – and I – in the park
simple past: in town – Sarah – on a fine day – to go shopping – last week
going to-future: in the kitchen – to cook dinner – we – at six o'clock
present perfect: to do – carefully – they – always – their homework

ÜBUNG 3 Ergänze die folgenden Sätze. Höre dir dazu Track 8 auf der CD an.

8

She bought a lot of clothes although   .

Jim was unfair so   .

I opened the window because   .

Mrs Walker wanted to come but   .

Rose likes to ski although   .

Mrs Craig wanted her pupils to be quiet but   .

The children are playing inside because   .

The kitchen looks a mess so   .

ÜBUNG 4 Übersetze die Sätze.

Meine Eltern kauften letztes Jahr ein Haus.

Fred lernt seit neun Jahren Spanisch.

Philipp und Greg kauften weder Blumen noch ein anderes Geschenk.

Jim räumt manchmal den Tisch ab *(to clear)*.

Ich kann morgen auf die Party gehen.

5.2 Verneinte Aussagesätze

Verneinte Aussagesätze werden analog den bejahten Aussagesätzen gebildet. Hinzu kommt der verneinende Zusatz *not*: **Subjekt + Hilfsverb + *not* + Vollverb + Ergänzungen**	I have not done my homework. I am not talking to you. They did not clean their rooms.
Es gibt verschiedene Hilfsverben: Die Formen von *to be, to have, to do* sowie die Modalverben *can, may* und *must*.	be → I am / was not going to India. have → I have not been to India. do → I do not / did not go to India. can → I cannot go to India.
Merke: must wird zu *need not / needn't* (↑ Kap. 2.3)!	must → I need not go to India.
Verneinte Zeitformen werden mit dem entsprechenden Hilfsverb + *not* + Vollverb gebildet: ▪ ***present progressive:*** *am / are / is* + not + Vollverb + *-ing* ▪ ***will-future:*** *will* + *not* + Vollverb ▪ ***going to-future:*** *am / are / is* + *not* + *going to* + Vollverb ▪ ***past progressive:*** *was / were* + *not* + Vollverb + *-ing* ▪ ***present perfect:*** *have / has* + *not* + *past participle* ▪ **Modalsätze:** Modalverb + *not* + Vollverb	They are not singing a song. He will not be happy. They are not going to meet their friends. Lisa was not wearing a hat. Tim has not tidied his room. I cannot go to school today. We must not go to the cinema at 10 p.m.
Aufgepasst: In Aussagesätzen im ***simple present*** benötigst du bei der Verneinung (außer bei *to be*) das Hilfsverb **to do** + not + Vollverb! Das verneinte ***simple past*** wird durch **did** + *not* + Vollverb angezeigt.	Frank speaks French. → Frank does not speak French. She is sad. → She is not sad. She wrote a letter. → She did not write a letter.
Achtung: Bei Negativwörtern wie *nobody, never* und *nothing* brauchst du kein zusätzliches *not* einsetzen.	Nobody came in. I have never been to the museum. I had nothing to do with it.

Der Satz

 ÜBUNG 5 Unterstreiche und kennzeichne in den folgenden bejahten Aussagesätzen alle Hilfsverben (Hv) und alle Vollverben (Vv).

Beispiel: They can go to the doctor. can (Hv) go /Vr)

He was sitting on the chair.

She went to bed early.

Christina has worked for two hours.

Lydia and Kim were having fun.

He wrote an e-mail.

Tina is eating a banana.

WISSEN

Die Kurzform der Verneinung
In der Schriftsprache verwendet man die Langform, in der gesprochenen Sprache meist die Kurzform der Hilfs- und Modalverben.

Aufgepasst: May not existiert nur in der Langform!

do / does not → don't / doesn't
did not → didn't
was / were not → wasn't / weren't
have / has not → haven't / hasn't
had not → hadn't
will not → won't
cannot → can't
could not → couldn't
must not → mustn't

 ÜBUNG 6 Verneine nun die Sätze aus Übung 5. Schreibe jeweils Kurz- und Langform.

5.2 Verneinte Aussagesätze

ÜBUNG 7 Bilde vollständige verneinte Sätze mit der angegebenen Zeit.

simple present: we – to go – to school

We don't go to school.

simple past: they – to listen – to music

simple past: Liz – to work – in the garden

simple present: Larry – to buy – a present

simple past: we – to watch – TV

simple past: I – to clean – the windows

simple present: she – to read – the book

simple present: they – to go – to the museum

ÜBUNG 8 Übersetze die folgenden Sätze. Schreibe in dein Übungsheft.

Tino ging gestern nicht nach Hause.
Niemand aß den Kuchen.
Walter und Ian nahmen nicht den Bus *(to take, past progressive)*.
Rita wird sich nicht mit Tina treffen *(going to-future)*.
Sie haben nie ein Buch gelesen.
Janice half ihrer Mutter nicht.

Der Satz

ÜBUNG 9 Bilde aus den folgenden Satzteilen verneinte Sätze.

simple present: can – mum – to cook

simple past: to jump – on the chair – I

present perfect: to read – she – for two weeks – a book

simple present: Charly – soon – must – go home *(Vorsicht)*

will-future: it – today – rain

going to-future: now – to sing – Freddy – for us

simple past: nobody – to sing – a song

present perfect: I – to school – to go – yet

simple present: may – to know – they – it

present perfect: to be – they – never – to France

will-future: they – to come

5.3 Bedingungssätze

Die Bildung von Bedingungssätzen

Bedingungssätze *(conditional sentences,* auch: *if-clauses)* beinhalten
- eine **Bedingung** und
- eine daraus abgeleitete **Folge**.

If you ring the bell, I will open the door.
If I pass the exam, I will be happy.
If you work too much, you will get tired.

Bedingungssätze bestehen aus einem *if*-Satz (Bedingung) + Hauptsatz (Folge). Die Reihenfolge dieser beiden Satzteile ist austauschbar.

Achtung: Steht der *if*-Satz an zweiter Stelle, entfällt das Komma!

If Tom runs, he will catch the bus.
Tom will catch the bus if he runs.

Achte auf die **Zeiten** in den beiden Satzteilen:
- Der *if*-Satz steht im **simple present**,
- der Hauptsatz wird mit dem **will-future** gebildet.

If Aunt Helen visits us, we will show her the house.
If Tim gets up early, he will catch the 9:30 train.

Der Unterschied zwischen *if* und *when*

If und **when** bedeuten beide *wenn*. Sie werden jedoch unterschiedlich gebraucht.

If kannst du auch mit *falls* übersetzen. Es handelt sich um eine **Bedingung,** die etwas zur Folge hat.

If Jane comes to the party, we will have fun. → Wenn / Falls Jane auf die Party kommt, dann werden wir Spaß haben (wenn sie nicht kommt, dann nicht).

Bei **when** ist ein **Zeitpunkt** gemeint, zu dem etwas geschehen wird. Anstatt *wenn* kann man auch *sobald* sagen.

When Jane comes to the party, we will start the game. → Wenn / Sobald Jane auf die Party kommt, fangen wir mit dem Spiel an (Jane hat gesagt, dass sie kommt, aber sie ist noch nicht da).

When-Sätze werden wie *if*-Sätze gebildet.

If mum arrives earlier, we will start cooking sooner.
When mum arrives, we will start cooking.

Der Satz

ÜBUNG 10 Füge die passende Verbform ein.

If Kim _____ (to visit) Tom, she _____ (to have) a good time.

If our team _____ (to win) the match, we _____ (to have) a big party.

If it _____ (to rain), Tim and Gina _____ (to go) by bus.

Mr Jones _____ (to catch) the 7:15 train if he _____ (to leave) immediately *(sofort)*.

If they _____ (to visit) Aunt Jill, they _____ (to see) the picture.

My parents _____ (to sell) our old car when they _____ (to buy) a new one.

If Simon _____ (to write) her an e-mail, Tina _____ (to be) happy.

If you _____ (to eat) too much chocolate, you _____ (to feel) bad.

WISSEN

Die Verneinung von Bedingungssätzen

- **verneinter *if*-Satz:** If it **doesn't** rain, we will go to the park.
  If you **aren't** honest *(ehrlich)*, you will get problems.

- **verneinter Hauptsatz:** If you drink coffee in the evening, you **will not / won't** sleep.
  If John forgets his homework, he **will not / won't** get a good mark.

- **beide Satzteile verneint:** If she **doesn't** come, she **will not / won't** see the show.
  If you **don't** eat the cake, you **will not / won't** get fat.

ÜBUNG 11 Bilde vollständige Bedingungssätze. Verbinde die *if*-Satzteile mit den passenden Hauptsatzteilen. Schreibe die Sätze in dein Übungsheft.

if-Satz

I (to tell) you the truth
you (not – to call) her
Susan (to stay) longer
you (to go) to bed early
we (to work) hard
he (not – to do) his homework

Hauptsatz

we (to get) good marks
you (to be) shocked
he (not – pass) the exams
she (to be) angry
she (to miss) the bus
you (not – to be) tired the next morning

5.3 Bedingungssätze

ÜBUNG 12 Fülle die Lücken mit den richtigen Zeitformen und entscheide, ob du *when* oder *if* einsetzen musst.

Mum _____ (to be) there _____ (Bedingung) you _____ (to arrive) at 7 o'clock.

_____ (Zeitpunkt) we _____ (to start) eating, you _____ (not – to talk) anymore.

Sally _____ (to read) the book _____ (Zeitpunkt) she _____ (to get) it.

Henry _____ (to win) the match _____ (Bedingung) Sandy _____ (not – to play) well.

_____ (Zeitpunkt) she _____ (to arrive) at the hotel, she _____ (to meet) him.

_____ (Bedingung) you _____ (to make) too many mistakes, you _____ (not – to pass) the exam.

ÜBUNG 13 Übersetze die Sätze ins Englische: *if* oder *when*?

Ich werde nach Hause gehen, wenn (sobald) es dunkel wird.

_____

Meine Mutter wird böse sein, wenn (falls) ich nicht komme.

_____

Mr Jordan wird die Hunde füttern, wenn (sobald) wir ihn bitten *(to ask)*.

_____

Simon wird nicht einkaufen gehen, wenn (falls) ihn seine Mutter nicht bittet.

_____

Wenn (sobald / falls) Tina die Nachricht *(message)* liest, wird sie unglücklich sein.

_____

85

Der Satz

5.4 Relativsätze

Die Bildung von Relativsätzen

Ein **Relativsatz** *(relative clause)* erweitert einen Satz, indem er Personen, Dinge oder Tiere näher beschreibt.

This is the man   who bought the car.
↓   ↓
Hauptsatz   Relativsatz

Relativsätze werden durch **Relativpronomen** eingeleitet:
◼ *who* und *that* beziehen sich auf Personen; die Objektform lautet *whom*,
◼ *which* und *that* beziehen sich auf Dinge oder Tiere,
◼ *whose* zeigt eine Zugehörigkeit oder ein Besitzverhältnis an („wessen?").

A doctor is a person **who** can help people.
This ist the teacher **whom** I like most.
This is the book **which** you gave me.

The man **whose** daughter won the competition is a teacher.

Die Verwendung von Relativsätzen

Ein **Relativsatz** *(relative clause)* bestimmt das Bezugswort näher. Einen Relativsatz, der für das Verständnis des gesamten Satzes notwendig ist, nennt man einen **notwendigen Relativsatz** *(defining relative clause)*.
Bei Personen steht *who / that*, bei Dingen und Tieren *which / that*.

This is the girl **who / that** lives next door.
Robert loves books **which / that** are exciting.

Ohne den Relativsatz wäre die Aussage des Hauptsatzes nicht vollständig: Es wäre nicht klar, wer oder was genau gemeint ist.

Merke: Es steht kein Komma vor dem Relativsatz!

Relativsätze mit und ohne Relativpronomen

Wird ein Relativpronomen in einem notwendigen Relativsatz als **Subjekt** („wer oder was?") verwendet, darf es **nicht weglassen** werden!

My grandma is an old lady **who** always wears a skirt.
(Wer trägt immer Röcke? → the old lady)

86

5.4 Relativsätze

Wird ein Relativpronomen in einem notwendigen Relativsatz als **Objekt** („wen oder was?") verwendet, **kann** es **weggelassen** werden.

My grandma is an old lady **who** I like very much.
(Wen mag ich? → the old lady)

Merke: Ein notwendiger Relativsatz ohne Relativpronomen heißt *contact clause*.

→ My grandma is an old lady I like very much.

Zur Probe, ob du das Relativpronomen weglassen kannst, musst du die **Subjekt- oder Objektfrage** stellen:
■ „wer oder was?" → Subjekt → das Relativpronomen muss stehen,

Gina is a person who eats a lot.
(„Wer isst viel?")
→ kein Weglassen von *who* möglich!

■ „wen oder was?"/ „wem?" → Objekt → das Relativpronomen kann entfallen.

Aber:
Gina is a person who you can trust.
(„Wem kannst du vertrauen?")
→ Weglassen von *who* ist möglich:
Gina is a person you can trust.

Achtung: In nicht notwendigen Relativsätzen darf *who* oder *which* **nicht** weggelassen werden!

My brother, **who** could help me, is on holiday.
We spent our holidays in London, **which** is a big city.

Präpositionen im notwendigen Relativsatz

In einem notwendigen Relativsatz kann eine Präposition stehen
■ vor dem Relativpronomen *who* oder *which*,

This is the pen **with which** I write at school.

■ am Ende des Satzes, wenn das Relativpronomen *that* ist,

This is the pen **that** I write at school **with.**

■ am Ende des Satzes in einem *contact clause*.

This is the pen   I write at school with.

Merke: Vor *that* steht niemals eine Präposition.

Ein Relativsatz kann durch *where* oder *when* eingeleitet werden, wenn das Bezugswort einen Ort oder einen Zeitpunkt angibt.

This is the house **in which** (= where) I live.
I give you the time **at which** (= when) we must leave.

87

Der Satz

 ÜBUNG 14 Relativpronomen leiten einen Relativsatz ein. Welche Relativpronomen kennst du und auf wen oder was beziehen sie sich?

h_____ :   w_____ :
P_____   D_____ oder T_____

t_____ :   w____ o____ :
P_____ , D_____ , T_____   zeigt eine Z_____ an

 ÜBUNG 15 Unterstreiche den Relativsatz und kreise das Relativpronomen ein.

This is the man who bought the car.

A Smart is a car which is small.

He is the boy who took the CD.

People who drive too fast are stupid.

These are the books that are cheap.

Ted, who found the money, is a young man.

5.4 Relativsätze

ÜBUNG 16 Setze das fehlende Relativpronomen ein.

This is the old lady   *whose*   garden I like.
Frederic is a boy _____ can sing and play the guitar.
Jason's mother is a nurse _____ works at General Hospital.
They showed a film _____ was brilliant.
This is Margret _____ aunt works in the bakery.
This is my friend Ron _____ I gave the book.
Mr Harold is the neighbour _____ dogs are always barking (*bellen*).
Mrs Richard is the teacher _____ went bungee jumping last year.

ÜBUNG 17 Beschreibe die folgenden Personen und Dinge näher. Verwende die angegebenen Satzteile, indem du das richtige Relativpronomen einsetzt.

A nurse is a person   *who helps people.*
A sheperd (*Schäfer*) is a person _____
A teacher is a person _____
A VW Beetle is a car _____
A lipstick is like a pen _____
Brad Pitt is an actor _____
A waiter is someone _____

Der Satz

ÜBUNG 18 Gib an, ob es sich bei dem Relativpronomen um ein Subjekt oder Objekt handelt und ob das Relativpronomen weggelassen werden kann!

1. Mr Brown is the police officer who asked the questions.
   Frage: **Wer** stellte die Fragen? → who (the police officer)

   ☐ Who wird als Subjekt gebraucht und kann nicht weggelassen werden.

   ☐ Who wird als Objekt gebraucht und kann weggelassen werden.

   Der Satz lautet dann:

2. Take the cheese that I bought yesterday.
   Frage: **Wen oder was** kaufte ich? → that (the cheese)

   ☐ That wird als Subjekt gebraucht und kann nicht weggelassen werden.

   ☐ That wird als Objekt gebraucht und kann weggelassen werden.

   Der Satz lautet dann:

ÜBUNG 19 Wird das Relativpronomen in den folgenden Sätzen als Objekt oder als Subjekt gebraucht? Wenn es als Objekt verwendet wird, kann man es weglassen – streiche es in diesem Fall durch.

This is the key which I was looking for.

Teresa helped grandma who was in hospital.

Mrs Rose is the teacher who Francis had in biology.

Take the shirt which is in the washing machine.

Take the cup which you like most.

Where is the CD that I got for my birthday?

This is the watch which is broken.

Luke likes the book which he has just read.

Anna loves the boy who sits next to her in class.

My father is a man who collects stamps.

5.4 Relativsätze

ÜBUNG 20 Finde den passenden Relativsatz. Wenn das Relativpronomen Objekt des Relativsatzes ist, lasse es weg.

- young and old people like
- are happy
- you can trust *(vertrauen)*
- works for a big company
- wrote a lot of novels
- Linda found last week
- was lying on the street
- I was using for my letter

Jane Austen is a British author ...

Volleyball is a team sport ...

I like people ...

Justin is a boy ...

It's Jim's box ...

Marion loves a man ...

Where is the pen ...

The car hit the tree ...

Der Satz

ÜBUNG 21 Höre dir Track 9 auf der CD an und ergänze die Sätze.

Can you see _____ is in front of the shop?

This is _____ helps me with my homework.

This is _____ I couldn't do.

Is this _____ CDs you like?

Have you got _____ is sharp enough for the bread?

Peter is _____ lives in Peru.

These are _____ daughter sings in a famous choir.

They stole _____ was in her jacket.

Is this _____ bark is worse than its bite?

Look at _____ are dancing over there!

ÜBUNG 22 Verbinde jeweils einen Satz aus der linken und rechten Spalte zu einem Hauptsatz und einem Relativsatz.

Gina's mother works for a company.	She is interested in art.
Queen Elizabeth doesn't have to pay the rent *(Miete)*.	He is sitting at the table next to us.
This is the old CD.	It was in my bag.
The old man is blind.	She lives in Buckingham Palace.
Babette is an old friend.	The company produces computers.

92

Klassenarbeit 1

Klassenarbeiten

 45 Minuten

AUFGABE 1 Bejahte und verneinte Aussagesätze: Ordne die einzelnen Satzteile in der richtigen Reihenfolge. Schreibe die Sätze in dein Übungsheft.

I / for four years / lived / in Berlin / have.
like / did / Dana / not / the show.
start / Francis / the race / cannot.
was / not / I / of the test / afraid.
wash / is / going to / Simon / the car.
was / she / cleaning / her bike / not.

AUFGABE 2 Setze das fehlende Bindewort ein.

He went to bed _____ (weil) he was tired.

You can _____ (entweder) have coffee _____ (oder) tea.

Tom doesn't talk to Pam _____ (obwohl) he likes her.

John didn't win the prize _____ (aber) the audience *(Publikum)* loved him.

This is _____ (weder) my dog _____ (noch) his dog.

AUFGABE 3 Falsche Satzstellung! Verbessere jeweils den ganzen Satz und schreibe ihn richtig in dein Übungsheft.

Always we go on Saturday evenings to the cinema.
Tim forgets never his keys.
My mother plays in the evening sometimes the piano.
We go skiing in winter often.

AUFGABE 4 Bilde verneinte Aussagesätze. Achte auf die richtige Zeit und schreibe Lang- und Kurzform. Schreibe die Sätze in dein Übungsheft.

to clean his bike / Frank *(simple past)*
to sit in the bar / she *(past progressive)*
to come / Tom *(going to-future)*
to see the bird / Betty *(present perfect)*
to listen to music / they *(simple past)*
to be a film star / I *(will-future)*
to buy a skirt / Sarah *(present perfect)*
to catch the thieves / the police *(simple past)*

Der Satz

 AUFGABE 5 Bedingungssätze bestehen aus einem Hauptsatz und einem *if*-Satz. Setze die fehlenden Verben in der richtigen Zeit ein.

Kevin _____ (to be) a good student if he _____ (to learn) more.
The cat _____ (to fall) down if it _____ (to stop / not).
If we _____ (to start) now, we _____ (to finish) at 12 o'clock.
If Sue _____ (to walk) faster, she _____ (to get / not) wet.
If you _____ (to wait) for me, I _____ (to help) you.

 AUFGABE 6 Setze die passenden Relativpronomen ein.

Is this your bike _____ is standing in front of the tree?
Give me the book _____ is on the shelf.
Can you show me the lady _____ bag this is?
This is my brother _____ works at the cinema.
Mrs Johnson is the lady _____ son lives in Canada.
Are you the boy _____ lives next door?

 AUFGABE 7 Wann kannst du das Relativpronomen weglassen? Trage es nur in den Sätzen ein, wo es nicht fehlen darf.

Look at the girl _____ is next to Peter.
Mum baked a cake _____ you will like a lot.
Take the plate _____ is clean.
This is the friend _____ can juggle (*jonglieren*).
Carina is reading the book _____ Tim was talking about.
Did you know the man _____ asked for some money?

 AUFGABE 8 Übersetze die folgenden Sätze und schreibe sie in dein Übungsheft.

Ruth und Kim sprachen gestern nicht mit mir.
Wenn du das Fahrrad reparierst, koche ich für dich.
Gina ist das Mädchen, das Basketball spielt.

Klassenarbeit 2

Klassenarbeiten

 45 Minuten

AUFGABE 9 Ergänze die folgende Tabelle, indem du entweder die richtige Zeitform einsetzt oder einen Satz mit den Satzteilen bildest.

Zeitform	Satz
	She often goes to school by bike.
simple past: Alan / to write letters / yesterday	
present perfect: the children / to eat ice cream	
	I am in a hurry.
past progressive: Clive / to play tennis	
	Maybe her friends will come next week.
	Mum has just come upstairs.
going to-future: we / to visit / Aunt Beth	

AUFGABE 10 In den folgenden Sätzen ist etwas mit der Satzstellung durcheinander geraten. Unterstreiche den Fehler und schreibe dann den Satz richtig.

We will meet at seven o'clock in front of the cinema.

The Millers go usually to France during their summer holidays.

Sue has been to London never.

Mary looked angrily at her dog.

At five o'clock we can meet on Friday.

95

Der Satz

 AUFGABE 11 Beende die folgenden Sätze. Die Konjunktion wird dir dabei behilflich sein.

> to be terrible storm – to go skiing – can swim really well – to be really expensive – to play football

I often go swimming but I never _____ .
It was snowing yesterday so we _____ .
I have just bought those jeans although they _____ .
We had to go inside because there _____ .
Joe started to swim when he was five so he _____ .

 AUFGABE 12 Ergänze die folgenden Sätze mit dem richtigen Relativpronomen. Es gibt mehrere Lösungen.

I like dogs _____ don't bark or bite.
I don't like people _____ talk all the time.
I don't like films _____ are about monsters.
I like books _____ are about wizards and fairies.
I like friends _____ don't tell lies.

 AUFGABE 13 Vervollständige die Sätze, indem du den Satzteil in der Klammer ins Englische übersetzt. Achte auf die Satzstellung.

Tim gave Jane (gestern einige seiner alten CDs) _____
_____ .

Judy is waiting (vor dem alten Haus auf Veronica) _____
_____ .

Rick has just written (einige Emails an seine Freunde) _____
_____ .

I'm looking (in meinem Zimmer nach meinem Handy) _____
_____ .

I (suche oft nach meinem Stift) _____
_____ .

96

Klassenarbeit 3

Klassenarbeiten

 45 Minuten

AUFGABE 14 Fülle die Lücken mit *if* oder *when*.

Is it okay _____ I open the window? _____ it is too cold, I'll close it at once.

_____ we get home, we'll have tea. I have already made the sandwiches.

Ben, you must phone us _____ you arrive in Liverpool.

I'll get you something to eat _____ you are hungry.

My parents will pick us up from Kate's house _____ we phone.

_____ you study for the next class test, you will get a good mark.

AUFGABE 15 Verbessere die Fehler in den folgenden Bedingungssätzen.

If you wait a minute, I go with you.

_____

It will be quicker if you will go by train.

_____

We will go swimming if the weather will be fine.

_____

When I go to bed after 10 o'clock, I will oversleep.

_____

AUFGABE 16 Was wirst du in den folgenden Situationen machen? Ergänze die Bedingungssätze mit deinen eigenen Ideen.

If I get a good mark in my English test, _____.

If I win the first prize in a competition, _____.

If I find a purse in the street, _____.

If I have an accident with my bike, _____.

If I'm hungry, _____.

If I'm too late for school, _____.

97

Der Satz

 AUFGABE 17 Setze die fehlenden Relativpronomen ein. Manchmal sind verschiedene Relativpronomen richtig.

This must be the actor _____ Ben always talks about.

This is the bird _____ has a broken wing.

I don't like the shoes _____ Victoria is wearing.

I was angry with my friend _____ sister was rude to me.

There is the school _____ I went to for four years.

Is this the part of the palace _____ burnt down last year?

 AUFGABE 18 Bilde einen Satz aus den jeweils zwei Sätzen. Wähle das richtige Relativpronomen, benutze kein Relativpronomen in *contact clauses*. Achte auf die richtige Satzstellung.

That's the disco. Robert met Sarah there.

_____

This is the snack bar. It is famous for its crisps.

_____

We saw the man. He lives in a huge house just across the road.

_____

This is my uncle. His name is Billy.

_____

Tim is a friend. I can trust him.

_____

 AUFGABE 19 Übersetze die folgenden Sätze. Schreibe in dein Übungsheft.

Falls es heftig schneit, wird der Direktor die Schule für zwei Tage schließen.
Sobald die Schule aus ist, laufen die meisten Kinder zur Bushaltestelle.
Fiona kennt nicht das Haus, in dem ihre Freundin wohnt.
Vor zwei Jahren haben wir unsere Ferien in Italien verbracht.
Gestern traf ich Sally gegen 3 Uhr in der Stadt.

6

Fragen

6.1 *Simple past* und *past progressive*

Die Bildung von Fragen im *simple past*

In der einfachen Vergangenheit *(simple past)* gibt es zwei Arten, eine Frage zu bilden:
- Fragen mit dem **Vollverb *to be***:
(Fragewort +) *was / were* + Subjekt
- Fragen mit **anderen Vollverben**:
(Fragewort +) *did* + Subjekt + Vollverb

Verneinte Fragen werden mit *was / were* + *not* oder *did* + *not* gebildet.

Were you ill?
How was the show?
Did she eat in the kitchen?
What did you do yesterday?

Wasn't she here yesterday?
Didn't you write me a letter?

Die Bildung von Fragen im *past progressive*

In der Verlaufsform der Vergangenheit *(past progressive)* wird eine Frage nur mit *was / were* gebildet:
- (Fragewort) + *was / were* + Subjekt + Vollverb
- Verneinte Fragen werden mit *was / were* + *not* gebildet.

Were they painting the room?
Was she having fun?
Where was Anna waiting?
Who was watching the movie?
Weren't you cleaning the kitchen?

Frageformen

Es gibt verschiedene Frageformen:
- Eine **Entscheidungsfrage** ist eine Frage ohne Fragewort. Es wird entweder „ja" oder „nein" erwartet.
Als Antwort gibst du eine Kurzantwort *(short answer)* (↑ S. 103).
- Eine **Ergänzungsfrage** ist eine Frage mit einem Fragewort. Sie fragt nach Informationen, die über „ja" und „nein" hinausgehen.
Bei der Antwort ist keine Kurzantwort möglich.

Were you hungry? – Yes, I was.
Weren't you tired yesterday? – No, I wasn't.
Was he walking alone? – Yes, he was.

Who was here? – Simon was here and brought some flowers.
What did you do? – I went to the shop.
Why was he running so fast? – He was late for school.

WISSEN

Fragen

Die wichtigsten **Fragewörter** sind:
what – was
where – wo / wohin
when – wann
who – wer / wen
why – warum
whose – wessen
how – wie

What were you doing?
Where is Patrick?
When did John leave the house?
Who is coming in?
Why were they angry?
Whose car is it?
How many bottles are left?

Ergänzungsfragen

Ergänzungsfragen fragen nach dem Subjekt oder nach anderen Satzteilen. Bei Fragen nach dem **Subjekt** *(who?)* steht
■ das Fragewort anstelle des Subjekts,
■ in verneinten Fragen *does / did*.

Bei Fragen nach anderen **Satzteilen**
■ ist die Satzstellung die gleiche wie im *simple present* (Fragewort + Hilfsverb + Subjekt + Vollverb),
■ steht *did* und *didn't* (im *simple present*: *do / does* und *don't / doesn't*).

Who visited grandma?
(„wer?" – der Enkel besuchte sie)
Who didn't pass the exam?
(„wer?" – John fiel durch die Prüfung)
What did you put on the table?
When did you leave school?
Where did he go? (Where does he go?)
Why didn't you go home?
(Why don't you go home?)

Question tags

Question tags sind **Frageanhängsel**, die mit *oder* oder *nicht wahr* übersetzt werden können.
■ Frage mit ***to be***: Im Frageanhängsel wird die entsprechende Form von *to be* wiederholt.
■ Frage mit einem **anderen Vollverb**: Im Frageanhängsel wird *did* benötigt.

Merke: Ein bejahter Satz erhält ein verneintes Frageanhängsel, ein verneinter Satz erhält ein bejahtes Frageanhängsel!

You passed the exam, didn't you? – Du hast die Prüfung bestanden, nicht wahr?

The pizza was good, wasn't it?
The pizza wasn't good, was it?

Frank worked hard, didn't he?
Frank didn't work hard, did he?

6.1 *Simple past* und *past progressive*

ÜBUNG 1 Hier sind sieben Fragewörter versteckt. Schreibe sie heraus und übersetze sie.

Z	W	B	Y	J	N	W	B
W	H	O	Q	Q	G	H	V
V	E	A	E	R	F	Y	Z
X	R	S	Z	G	L	H	I
H	E	W	H	O	S	E	Z
O	U	R	R	A	O	C	C
W	H	E	N	W	B	H	J
U	M	R	H	W	H	A	T

What = was
Why = warum
Who = wer
Where = wo
When = wann
Whose = wessen
How = wie

ÜBUNG 2 Wandle die Fragen vom *simple present* in das *simple past* um. Schreibe die Sätze in dein Übungsheft.

Where are you?   Whose jeans are these?
Who goes to school?   When does the shop open?
How are they?   What books do you like?
Why do you like potatoes?   Who is your favourite actor?

ÜBUNG 3 Setze die einzelnen Sätze in die Frageform und achte auf die richtige Zeit.

Mum bought a book.   Who did bought a book?

He was going to school.   Who was going to school?

They were afraid of the test. *Angst haben* Who were afraid of the test?

You studied for the test.   Who studied for the test?

ÜBUNG 4 Ersetze in folgenden Ergänzungsfragen die roten Satzteile mit einem Fragewort und formuliere die ganze Frage.

John slept until noon.   Who slept until noon?

Jonathan went to Hamburg.   Where to Jonathan went?

Jimmy sat on the chair.   Who sat on the chair?

He played football on Saturday.   When he played football?

This was Jimmy's bike.   Who was this bike?

101

Fragen

> ### WISSEN +
>
> **Fehlerquelle: *was/were* oder *did*?**
> Achte genau darauf, ob im Ausagesatz
> ■ *was/were* steht: Dann bildest du auch die Frage mit *was/were*.
> ■ ein Vollverb steht: Dann musst du die Frage mit *did* bilden.
>
> *Aufgepasst:* Das *simple past* wird bereits durch das *did* ausgedrückt, deshalb folgt das Vollverb **immer** in der Grundform!
>
> He was happy. → Was he happy?
> You were at home. → Were you at home?
> You cleaned the door. → Did you clean the door?
> She looked at you. → Did she look at you?

 ÜBUNG 5 Achte auf die Satzfragmente und bilde Entscheidungsfragen im *simple past*. Schreibe in dein Übungsheft.

Beispiel: to be hungry – they → Were they hungry?

to sit in the park – she
to help grandma – you
to write an e-mail – not – he
to be hungry – you
to listen to a CD – they
to be alone – he
to be old – they
to go skating – you
to be ready – they
to fly to Rome – not – he

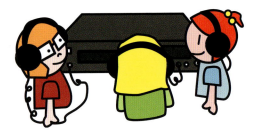

 ÜBUNG 6 Die folgenden Sätze enthalten viele Informationen. Formuliere verschiedene Fragen nach den einzelnen Satzteilen.

1. Frank visited his aunt in Birmingham.

   Who
   What
   Who
   Where

102

6.1 *Simple past* und *past progressive*

2. Sandra and Jenny saw an old lady in the park who looked very sad.

Who
What
What / Who
Where
Who
How

ÜBUNG 7 Wandle die folgenden Satzfragmente in eine *simple past*-Frage und danach in eine *past progressive*-Frage um. Schreibe in dein Übungsheft.

Beispiel: to watch TV – she → Did she watch TV? Was she watching TV?

to take pictures – you
to play volleyball – not – they
to go to the concert – he
to have fun – you
to buy a present – we
to write an essay – not – Tim

WISSEN

Kurzantworten
Bei Entscheidungsfragen genügt es nicht, nur *yes* oder *no* zu sagen. Man braucht immer eine **Kurzantwort** *(short answer)*.
Steht in der Frage *was / were*, wird auch mit *was / were* geantwortet.
Steht in der Frage *did* + Vollverb, wird auch mit ***did*** geantwortet.

Was she ill? – Yes, she was.
Were they on holiday? – No, they were not / weren't.

Did they go to Spain? – Yes, they did.
Did you leave a message? – No, I didn't.

103

Fragen

 ÜBUNG 8 Beantworte die Fragen mit einer Kurzantwort. Antworte jeweils mit „ja" und mit „nein". Schreibe die Antworten in dein Übungsheft.

Did he buy the green shirt?
Did they play basketball?
Were you at the party?

Was she having fun all day long?
Was he sad?
Was the cat sitting next to us?

WISSEN

Question tags (Frageanhängsel)
Bei den *question tags* gelten die Regeln der Kurzantworten (↑ S. 103):
was / were → wasn't / weren't
andere Vollverben → did!

Merke: Positive Aussage → negatives Frageanhängsel,
negative Aussage → positives Frageanhängsel!

You were at the party, weren't you?
He played the guitar, didn't he?
She wasn't at school, was she?
She didn't call, did she?

 ÜBUNG 9 Ergänze die richtigen *question tags*.

They weren't sitting in the kitchen,   ?

It rained in the afternoon,   ?

She didn't clean the room,   ?

Georgia wasn't in the hospital,   ?

They talked to Harry,   ?

 ÜBUNG 10 Höre dir Track 10 auf der CD an und ergänze das fehlende Fragewort.

         bought the shoes?

         did Jane come home?

         long has Gwen been living in Wales?

         are you late again?

         can I put my coat?

         often has Robert phoned so far?

         are you going to invite to your party?

6.1 *Simple past* und *past progressive*

WISSEN

some und *any*

Some wird in **bejahten Aussagesätzen** verwendet sowie in **höflichen Fragen**, **Vorschlägen** und **Antworten** benutzt; vor allem dann, wenn der Sprecher eine positive Antwort erwartet.

I bought some apples.
Would you like to have some biscuits? –
Yes, of course.

Any wird in **verneinten Aussagesätzen** und in **Fragen** verwendet.
Im bejahten Aussagesatz bedeutet *any* jeder / jedes Beliebige.

She couldn't buy any apples.
Have you got any problems?
You can read any book you like.

Diese Regeln gelten auch für zusammengesetzte Formen mit *some* und *any*.

somebody, someone, something, somewhere
anybody, anyone, anything, anywhere

ÜBUNG 11 Vervollständige die Sätze mit *some* oder *any* und dem passenden Gegenstand.

presents | books | fun | milk | meat | some / any

I love to read. Have you got _____ ?

Tina is vegetarian. She doesn't like _____ .

Here is your tea. But I'm sorry, I haven't got _____ .

Let's have a party. I want to have _____ .

Soon it's Christmas. Have you already bought _____ ?

ÜBUNG 12 Setze die passende Form von *some*, *any* oder einer Zusammensetzung ein.

Verena wants to buy _____ apples. – He has lost his keys _____ . – Can _____ help me? – Are there _____ eggs left? – She hasn't got _____ to say. – I am wearing _____ new. – It was dark. I didn't see _____ . – Let's make _____ sandwiches. – Where are my keys? I can't find them _____ .

105

Fragen

6.2 *Present perfect*

Frageformen

Beim einfachen Perfekt *(present perfect)* gibt es wie beim *simple past* verschiedene Frageformen (↑ Kap. 6.1):

■ **Entscheidungsfragen** *(ja / nein)* und

Have you heard the news? – Yes, I have. / No, I haven't.
Have you been to Ireland? – Yes, I have. / No, I haven't.

■ **Ergänzungsfragen** (weitere Informationen).

Where have you been? – I have been to Switzerland.
What have you learned today? – We have learned some new words.

Die Bildung von Fragen im *present perfect*

Beim *present perfect* werden die Fragen immer mit *to have* gebildet:
(Fragewort +) *have / has* + Subjekt + *past participle*

Have you ever been to Iceland?
Where has she learned English?

Die **Kurzantworten** werden beim *present perfect* immer mit dem Hilfsverb *to have* gebildet.

Have you seen my purse? –
Yes, I have. / No, I haven't.
Hasn't he read the newspaper? –
Yes, he has. / No, he hasn't.

Auch die **Frageanhängsel** werden mit *have / has* gebildet.

You have read this book, haven't you?
He hasn't got any money, has he?

Merke: Auch hier erfordert eine positive Aussage ein negatives Frageanhängsel und eine negative Aussage ein positives Frageanhängsel!

Aufgepasst: Die Zeitangaben *already – schon* (im bejahten Satz) und *just – gerade eben* stehen in der Frage nach dem Subjekt und vor dem *past participle*.
Yet – schon (im verneinten Satz) und *so far – bis jetzt, bisher* dagegen stehen am Ende des Satzes!

Have you already seen the new horror film?
Has he just turned off the light?

Where have you been so far?
Haven't you done the washing-up yet?

WISSEN

106

6.2 *Present perfect*

ÜBUNG 13   Setze das passende Fragewort ein.

_____ has Kim been so far?	_____ has helped Jim since April?
_____ have you been to Paris?	_____ car have they stolen?

ÜBUNG 14   Die folgenden Sätze sind nicht vollständig. Frage nach dem fehlenden Satzteil und benutze das *present perfect*.
Beispiel: They have learned ... since May. → What have they learned since May?

... has been to Russia. → _____ ?

Simon has left his ... at school. → _____ ?

Mr Finn has been in ... for five months. → _____ ?

John and Steve have slept too long because ... . → _____
_____ ?

... has not called yet. → _____ ?

ÜBUNG 15   Formuliere Fragen aus den Satzbausteinen.

travelled / he / has / where / so far   you / listened / have / yet / to the CD
just / Betty / what / has / read   have / I / seen / haven't I / you
Spanish / Richard / learned / has / for a long time

ÜBUNG 16   Übersetze. Schreibe die Lösungen in dein Übungsheft.

Warst du schon in Paris?
Du hast die Küche nicht geputzt, oder *(question tag)*?
David, hast du Clare gesehen?
Wo hat Fred bisher gearbeitet?
Mr Keller ist nicht nach Japan geflogen, oder doch *(question tag)*?
Hat Vater schon angerufen?

Fragen

Klassenarbeit 1

⏱ 45 Minuten

 AUFGABE 1 Setze das passende Fragewort ein. Schreibe in Klammern, um welche Zeitform es sich handelt: *simple past, past progressive* oder *present perfect*.

Where	have they been since July?	**(present perfect)**
	did you watch on TV last night?	
	called the police?	
	was Tina painting the room?	
	long did you stay in Spain?	

 AUFGABE 2 Wandle die Frage in die angegebene Zeitform um.

Where are you? *(simple past)*

Does Kim sit next to you? *(past progressive)*

Where do you work? *(present perfect)*

Is mum crying? *(past progressive)*

When must they leave the party? *(simple past)*

 AUFGABE 3 Frage nach den roten Satzteilen.
Schreibe die Fragen in dein Übungsheft.

They were having fun at the party.
Steve sat on the chair.
They watched TV.
Jane wrote the e-mail yesterday.
Grandpa was unhappy because he lost the game.
Harry's bike was dirty.
Gina was playing a computer game.

108

Klassenarbeiten

AUFGABE 4 Formuliere die passende Entscheidungsfrage und gib bei „+" eine positive und bei „–" eine negative Kurzantwort.

Beispiel: to rain – it – *past progressive* (–) → Was it raining? – No, it wasn't.

to fly to Los Angeles – Jack → *simple past* (+)
to live in London – you → *present perfect* (–)
to sell a car – he → *past progressive* (+)
to call the police – the old lady → *simple past* (–)
to read a lot of books – he → *present perfect* (–)

AUFGABE 5 Bilde aus den folgenden Satzfragmenten Sätze mit Frageanhängseln.

simple past: to listen to the CD – she

  She listened to the CD, didn't she?

present perfect: not – to play golf – they

past progressive: to watch the movie – Vicky

simple past: to see a ghost – Zara

present perfect: not – to know the thief – Jack

simple past: to call the ambulance – the policeman

past progressive: to steal the bike – Luke

Fragen

Klassenarbeit 2

 45 Minuten

 AUFGABE 6 Finde das richtige Frageanhängsel *(question tag)* für die folgenden Aussagen.

Tony played football two years ago,

Mr Smith hasn't phoned yet,

The children were singing Irish folk songs,

You didn't write those stories yesterday,

Elaine wasn't driving to Cardiff,

Robert and Lisa haven't been to Wales yet,

Dad is watching TV,

Peter, you didn't buy some milk,

 AUFGABE 7 Finde zu den unterstrichenen Satzteilen der folgenden Aussagesätze die richtigen Fragen. Achte dabei auf die Zeitform der Aussagesätze.

Tim <u>was reading</u> comics yesterday afternoon.

Kim got up <u>at six o'clock</u> on Saturday.

The pupils in my class have just finished <u>their project on animals</u>.

<u>My dog</u> has already eaten all the dog biscuits.

I saw an exciting films <u>last weekend</u>.

The boys were swimming <u>in the cold lake</u>.

<u>The Millers</u> arrived too late.

Klassenarbeiten

AUFGABE 8 Bilde aus den vorgegebenen Satzteilen Fragen in der richtigen Zeit. Schreibe in dein Übungsheft.

simple past:
to be nervous – Tim
to buy the present – who
to buy the present – she – where
to sing – the pop star – many songs

present perfect:
to live in Sweden – they
to be – Tina – where

past progressive:
to read – she
to take pictures – she

AUFGABE 9 Übersetze die folgenden Sätze.

Wo verlor Mrs Green ihre Tasche?

Wann kam der Zug an *(to arrive)*?

Ich erzählte dir die Geschichte, oder nicht?

Las er das Buch? – Nein.

Spielten die Kinder im Garten?

Mr Smith ging gestern nicht zur Arbeit, nicht wahr?

Wer hat dieses Buch noch nicht gelesen?

7

Englisch lernen

7.1 Mit dem Wörterbuch umgehen

Zweisprachige Wörterbücher:
Sie sind zweiteilig. In der einen Hälfte findest du die Übersetzung vom Englischen ins Deutsche, in der anderen die Übersetzung vom Deutschen ins Englische.

Englisch-Deutsch:
abbreviation [əbriːvɪˈeɪʃn]: Abkürzung
Deutsch-Englisch:
Abkürzung: a) (Weg) short cut; b) (Wort) abbreviation

Einsprachige Wörterbücher:
Vorteil: Das englische Wort wird nur auf Englisch erläutert; du lernst so die Fremdsprache besser, da du ausschließlich mit englischen Wörtern arbeitest.

Nachteil: Du kannst damit nicht vom Deutschen ins Englische übersetzen.

to roar: to make a loud and deep sound (a lion roars)
pinkie: the smallest finger of a person's hand
lollipop: a sweet on a small stick

Für die Arbeit mit dem Wörterbuch solltest du
■ das **Alphabet** perfekt beherrschen,
■ alle **Abkürzungen** verstehen,
■ die **phonetische Lautschrift** verstehen.

Kommt *r* vor *v* oder nach *v*?
adj. = adjective
[ʃ] = „sch"

Anhand der Lautschrift erfährst du die Aussprache eines Wortes. Sie steht in eckigen Klammern hinter dem englischen Wort.

house [haʊs], brother [ˈbrʌðə(r)], me [mɪ], example [ɪgˈzɑːmpl]

Die meisten Wörterbücher haben einen **Anhang**. Hier findest du oft
■ eine Grundgrammatik,

■ eine Liste unregelmäßiger Verben,
■ Vorschläge für Briefformulierungen,
■ einen Überblick über die englischen und deutschen Maße und Gewichte, Zahlen, Datums- und Uhrzeitangaben.

Nomen, Verben (*simple past, simple present* ...), Demonstrativpronomen ...
irregular verbs: to go → went → gone
"Dear Sally, ..."
1 mile = 1,61 km, 1 gallon = 4,546 l
February 21st = 21. Februar

WISSEN

112

7.1 Mit dem Wörterbuch umgehen

ÜBUNG 1 Um rasch ein Wort im Wörterbuch zu finden, musst du fit im Alphabet sein.

1. Trage den Buchstaben davor und danach ein. Beispiel: <u>A</u> B <u>C</u>

| _ K _ | _ S _ | _ F _ | _ P _ | _ N _ | _ X _ |
| _ E _ | _ U _ | _ T _ | _ D _ | _ I _ | _ L _ |

2. Wie heißt der drittnächste Buchstabe? Beispiel: V <u>Y</u>

| D _ | T _ | J _ | C _ | I _ | O _ | N _ | E _ |
| S _ | Q _ | W _ | H _ | B _ | A _ | M _ | L _ |

3. Wie heißt der vorletzte Buchstabe? Beispiel: <u>F</u> H

| P _ | M _ | E _ | X _ | L _ | O _ | D _ | J _ |
| R _ | Z _ | N _ | S _ | W _ | T _ | F _ | C _ |

WISSEN

Wörter im Wörterbuch finden
Ein Tipp zum schnelleren Auffinden eines gesuchten Wortes im Wörterbuch: Auf der linken Seite oben steht immer das erste Wort der Seite, auf der rechten Seite oben steht immer das letzte Wort der Seite. Diese Wörter heißen Leitwörter. So weißt du, welche Wörter auf dieser Seite dazwischen vorkommen.

ÜBUNG 2 Im Folgenden stehen die beiden Leitwörter einer Seite im Wörterbuch. Unterstreiche die Wörter, die dazwischen passen.

dumpling – ear: Dutch – dweller – eagle – edge – dualism – dusty – dump
headliner – heel: Hebrew – heavy – heftily – headship – hazard – hearty
meet – merrily: mental – meekly – medium – middle – meteor – menagerie
ideal – illusionist: illegally – illustrate – idol – idea – idiotic – identical – icy

ÜBUNG 3 Suche die Übersetzung der rot markierten Wörter in einem Wörterbuch und schreibe sie neben die deutschen Wörter.

rain:	Regentropfen	Regenbogen
light:	Feuerzeug	Leuchtturm
fish:	Fischstäbchen	Fischer
back:	Rucksack	Hintergrund

113

Englisch lernen

 ÜBUNG 4 Hier werden dir unbekannte Wörter auf Englisch erklärt. Finde die richtige deutsche Übersetzung.

gag – joke or funny story →

desert – land with very little water and a lot of sand (the Sahara Desert)
→

locker – cupboard where clothes can be put in (for example at a swimming-pool)
→

nickname – short form of a name (Michael → Mike) →

to kneel – to go down on your knees →

foal – a young horse →

dormitory – large room with many beds →

chum – good old friend →

WISSEN

Die phonetische Lautschrift
Eine Besonderheit aller Wörterbücher ist die phonetische Lautschrift. Sie gibt an, wie ein Wort ausgesprochen wird. Es werden normale Buchstaben, aber auch besondere Zeichen verwendet. Merke dir die besonderen Zeichen am besten anhand eines einfachen Wortes!
Das englische Alphabet kennst du bereits aus Klasse 5. Du solltest es ständig wiederholen, damit du schnell buchstabieren kannst. Präge dir besonders *a*, *e* und *i* ein.

a [eɪ]	e [iː]	i [aɪ]	m [em]	q [kjuː]	u [juː]	y [waɪ]
b [biː]	f [ef]	j [dʒeɪ]	n [en]	r [ɑː(r)]	v [viː]	z [zed]
c [siː]	g [dʒiː]	k [keɪ]	o [əʊ]	s [es]	w [ˈdʌbljuː]	
d [diː]	h [eɪtʃ]	l [el]	p [piː]	t [tiː]	x [eks]	

[ŋ]	sing	[ɑː]	father	[aɪ]	fine, my
[r]	rose	[ʌ]	but, under	[aʊ]	now, house
[s]	class	[e]	pen	[eə]	there, pair
[z]	is	[ə]	a sister	[eɪ]	name, lay
[ʒ]	television	[ɜː]	girl	[ɪə]	here, nearly
[dʒ]	Germany, page	[æ]	fat	[ɔɪ]	boy
[ʃ]	ship	[ɪ]	bit	[əʊ]	old, hello
[tʃ]	chair, lunch	[iː]	easy, meet	[ʊə]	you're
[ð]	the	[ɒ]	got, on		
[θ]	thanks	[ɔː]	ball		
[v]	video, have	[ʊ]	book		
[w]	word, one	[uː]	too, two		

7.1 Mit dem Wörterbuch umgehen

ÜBUNG 5 Mit deinem Wissen über die phonetische Lautschrift kannst du nun die folgenden Wörter erkennen.

['suːpəmɑːkɪt] →

['neɪbə(r)] →

['bʌkɪt] →

['taɪmteɪbl] →

['vedʒɪtəbl] →

['hedeɪk] →

['prɒbəblɪ] →

WISSEN

Abkürzungen
Da jedes Wörterbuch Tausende von Wörtern besitzt, muss jeder Eintrag kurz gehalten werden. Deshalb werden viele Abkürzungen verwendet. Mach dich mit den Abkürzungen in deinem Wörterbuch vertraut! Ein Abkürzungsverzeichnis findest du meist vor dem Wörterverzeichnis.

ÜBUNG 6 Finde heraus, was die Abkürzungen bedeuten könnten.

complex: 1. **adj** kompliziert; 2. **n** Komplex

→ **adj** = _____ , **n** = _____

men: **pl of** man

→ **pl of** = _____

receive: **vb** erhalten; empfangen

→ **vb** = _____

lift: *n* Aufzug (**Brit.**)

→ (**Brit.**) = _____

elevator: *n* Aufzug (**Amer.**)

→ (**Amer.**) = _____

¹elder: *n* Ältere

²elder: *n* Holunder

→ ¹/² = _____

115

Englisch lernen

7.2 Hörverstehen

Bevor du den Text hörst

Wenn du den Text einer Hörverstehensaufgabe anhörst, musst du nicht jedes Wort kennen bzw. verstehen, um die Aufgaben bearbeiten zu können. Manchmal kannst du die Bedeutung eines Wortes aus dem Zusammenhang erschließen.

Hier sind noch einige Tipps, die du beachten solltest:

Lies dir die Aufgabenstellung genau durch, um herauszufinden, ob du Lücken füllen musst, du die richtige Antwort ankreuzen sollst oder ob Fragen zu beantworten sind.

Beim Durchlesen der Aufgabenstellung solltest du dich auch auf die **Art des Textes** einstellen, der in der Übung präsentiert wird. Es kann sich z. B. um einen Brief, einen Bericht oder ein Telefongespräch handeln.
Stelle dich auch auf die **Thematik** ein (ein Text über ein Land, eine Diskussion zu einer bestimmten Thematik).

Diese Vorüberlegungen sind hilfreich, weil du dir bereits **Vokabeln oder Formulierungen zurechtlegen** kannst, die du bei der Bearbeitung benötigst.

Merke: Manchmal ist es auch hilfreich, wenn du dir eine Tabelle oder Liste anlegst.

Wähle für deine Notizen für dich verständliche Abkürzungen und Symbole, damit du nicht immer vollständige Sätze schreiben musst – das ist zeitlich meist nicht möglich.
Sicherlich hast du auch viele eigene Ideen, wie du deine Notizen kurzhalten kannst.

Höre dir das folgende Telefonat zweimal an und beantworte folgende Fragen.
Höre dir den folgenden Text an und kreuze die richtigen Antworten an.

Kim: Kim speaking.
Sarah: Hi Kim. Have you got a few minutes?
Kim: Yes, sure. What's the matter?
Sarah: Well, you know it's Robert's birthday next week and he's is going to have a party on Saturday.
Kim: I would never forget Robert's birthday.

on the telephone – speaking
birthday – to have a party – invitation – present

Großbuchstaben für Namen oder Eigennamen: S für Sam, M für Max,
GB für Great Britain, Ger für Germany.
Einen Pfeil (→), wenn du zum Beispiel die Folge einer Handlung beschreiben möchtest: S played football → broke his arm.

WISSEN

116

Während du den Text hörst

Konzentriere dich auf den Text und auf das, was du hörst.

Gerate nicht in Panik, wenn du ein Wort oder einen Ausdruck nicht gleich verstehst. In einem Gespräch mit einem Briten oder Amerikaner wirst du auch nicht jedes einzelne Wort verstehen.
Versuche den Inhalt des Textes als Ganzes zu erfassen.

Mache dir auf einem Extrablatt **Notizen,** d. h., schreibe die Schlüsselwörter auf, die für die Beantwortung der Fragen wichtig sind. Manchmal helfen dir auch Symbole oder Abkürzungen, damit du keine Zeit verlierst.

Who? → Kim and Sarah
About what? → Robert's birthday
When? → on Saturday

Ergänze beim zweiten Hördurchgang Informationen, die dir fehlen.
Einige Hörverstehensaufgaben sind auch so angelegt, dass sie gleich beantwortet werden können. Dies gilt besonders für Ankreuzaufgaben.

Nachdem du den Text gehört hast

Beantworte in aller Ruhe die Fragen und **formuliere die Antworten in korrektem Englisch**. Achte dabei besonders auf die Satzstellung, die Zeitformen des Verbs und die Rechtschreibung.

Who is on the phone?
Sarah and Kim are on the phone.

Wähle bei der Beantwortung der Fragen immer die Zeitform, die auch in der Fragestellung verwendet wurde.

What are they talking about?
They are talking about Robert's birthday.

When is Robert going to have his party?
He is going to have his party on Saturday.

Wenn du dir noch immer unsicher bist, dann höre dir die CD noch einmal an – aber erst, wenn du alle Fragen zu einer Hörverstehensaufgabe bearbeitet hast.

Englisch lernen

ÜBUNG 7 Höre dir Track 11 auf der CD an und schreibe die fehlenden Wörter in die Lücken.

Hello, my name is Claire and I would like to talk about my school and _____ .

I have been going to a _____ in Glasgow since last summer.

My school is very big and there are about 900 _____ . I like it there and I

have already become friendly with some of the girls. I'm in _____

6 and I'm in the same _____ for all my _____ . You can learn two

_____ at my school: _____ or _____ . My favourite

subjects are _____ and P.E., which is _____ .

The first _____ is at ten to nine. On Monday we have _____

and after that _____ from 9:50 a.m. to 10:50 a.m. Then there is a

_____ and after that we have _____ and _____ .

_____ is from 1:10 p.m. to 2:10 p.m. and you can buy something to eat in

the _____ or you can bring a _____ . We have

_____ lessons from 2:10 p.m. to 3:20 p.m.

After the afternoon lessons have finished I sometimes stay for my _____ –

I play _____ every Wednesday.

ÜBUNG 8 Höre dir Track 12 auf der CD an – auch zwei- oder dreimal. Kreuze an, ob die Sätze richtig oder falsch sind. Korrigiere die, die nicht richtig sind, in deinem Übungsheft.

	right	wrong
1. Max is going to visit Sam during his Easter holidays.	☐	☐
2. Sam has got a brother called George and a sister called Janet.	☐	☐
3. George is older than Sam.	☐	☐
4. Sam is good at German.	☐	☐
5. Sam revises his German vocabulary regularly.	☐	☐
6. Sam hopes that the weather will be fine around Easter.	☐	☐
7. Max should bring along his roller skates.	☐	☐
8. Max has been playing tennis for about three years.	☐	☐

7.2 Hörverstehen

ÜBUNG 9 Höre dir Track 13 auf der CD zweimal an und kreuze die richtigen Aussagen an. Bevor du dir den Text anhörst, lies dir die Liste der Vokabeln durch, die dir helfen können, den Text besser zu verstehen.

crusade – Kreuzzug
to rule, ruled, ruled – herrschen, regieren
battle – Schlacht
mean – gemein
tax – Steuern
prison – Gefängnis

King Richard went away on a crusade

☐ in 1190.   ☐ in 1181.   ☐ in 1191.   ☐ in 1119.

Prince John ruled for his brother King Richard because

☐ he hated him.   ☐ he was away for a long time.
☐ he wanted to be king.   ☐ King Richard was dead.

Prince John was

☐ a nice person.   ☐ a boring person.
☐ a funny person.   ☐ a mean person.

Robin Hood's real name was

☐ Lord Nocksley.   ☐ Earl Locksley.   ☐ Lord Mocksley.   ☐ Lord Locksley.

When Robin Hood came back from the crusade,

☐ he had no father and no land.   ☐ his wife was dead.
☐ his friends hid in Sherwood Forest. ☐ the Sheriff of Nottingham was ill.

Robin Hood and his men lived in Sherwood Forest and

☐ he formed an army there.   ☐ they built a new castle there.
☐ they climbed trees there.   ☐ they killed the Sheriff of Nottingham there.

Englisch lernen

7.3 Englisch sprechen

Eine gute Methode, Englisch zu lernen, ist es, zu lesen oder Sätze nachzusprechen. Noch besser jedoch ist es, selbst aktiv zu werden.

Versuche ab jetzt, mehr Englisch zu sprechen
- im Unterricht,
- in der Pause mit deinen Mitschülern und Mitschülerinnen
- oder mit Touristen in der Stadt.

Could you repeat this, please?
Could you give me your pencil, please?

Can I help you? May I show you the way?

Nutze jede Gelegenheit zu sprechen, dann wird dir Englisch viel leichter fallen.

Tipp: Hab keine Angst vor Fehlern, denn aus Fehlern kann man lernen. Je häufiger du Englisch sprichst, liest oder schreibst, desto vertrauter wirst du mit der Sprache. Achte auf die **passenden Zeiten:**
- In diesem Augenblick Stattfindendes: *present progressive*
- Wiederkehrendes: *simple present* (*he / she / it* → das *s* muss mit!)
- Vergangenes: *simple past*
- Bis jetzt Andauerndes: *present perfect*
- Zukunft: *will-* oder *going to-future*

Tina is cleaning her bike now.

Mrs Jay always works in the garden.

I went to the cinema yesterday.
We have learned English for two years.
Henry is going to meet Astrid tomorrow.

Achte auf die **Satzstellung:**
- **Aussagen:** Subjekt (+ Hilfsverb) + Vollverb
- **Verneinungen:** Subjekt + Hilfsverb + *not* + Vollverb
- **Fragen:** (Fragewort +) Hilfsverb (+ *not*) + Subjekt + Vollverb

We (can) help in the kitchen.

Tina wasn't walking home.
George didn't go to the park.
Why are you singing this song?
Did Dana write an e-mail?
Why didn't you go to school yesterday?

WISSEN

7.3 Englisch sprechen

ÜBUNG 10 Verbinde jeweils eine Frage mit der passenden Antwort.

Whose book is this?
What's the time, please?
What's for homework?
How do you do this exercise?
Can you play the CD again, please?
Can I work with Steven?
Who's next?

Read the text on page eleven.
No, you have to work by yourself (*allein*).
It's mine.
It's Dan's turn.
Let me help you.
It's ten o'clock.
Yes, of course. But listen carefully now!

ÜBUNG 11 Bilde aus den folgenden Wörtern Sätze.

you / I think / right / are

I think

do / have / what / to do / we

is / think / it / boring / it / is / exciting / not / I

on / read / eleven / the text / page

exercise book / forgotten / have / I / my / sorry

ÜBUNG 12 Übersetze die folgenden Sätze. Achte besonders auf die Satzstellung! Schreibe in dein Übungsheft.

Kann ich auf die Toilette gehen / hinausgehen?
Kann ich bitte eine Frage stellen?
Können Sie es an die Tafel (*board*) schreiben?
Das glaube ich auch.
Ist das richtig? Ich bin mir nicht sicher.

Englisch lernen

7.4 Besser lesen und verstehen

Texte lesen und verstehen ist nicht immer einfach. Oft tauchen Wörter auf, die du nicht kennst.

Tipp: Um einen Text zu erfassen, ist es nicht nötig, jedes einzelne Wort zu kennen. Versuche einfach, **den Text insgesamt** zu verstehen!

Dann kannst du einzelne unbekannte **Wörter aus dem Zusammenhang** erschließen.

Man kann **einen Text auf verschiedene Arten** lesen:
▪ den Text überfliegen und sich einen ersten Eindruck verschaffen,
▪ bestimmte Information im Text suchen,
▪ den gesamten Inhalt erfassen und verstehen.

Versuche, einen Text wie ein Detektiv zu erschließen:
▪ Finde Informationen und
▪ versuche, einzelne Wörter nach und nach zu verstehen.

Aufgepasst: Bevor du ein Wörterbuch zur Hand nimmst, versuche erst, die Bedeutung des gesuchten Wortes selbst herauszufinden:
▪ aus dem Textzusammenhang,

▪ durch ein schon bekanntes ähnliches Wort aus der Wortfamilie,

▪ durch die Ähnlichkeit mit einem deutschen Wort.

In the sports shop I bought a *fraghwert*. It looks like a kind of ski but it is different: It's shorter and broader, and you can stand on it with two feet.

What do you think is a *fraghwert*?

Das Wort *fraghwert* kannst du nicht kennen, denn es ist ein Fantasiewort. Aber durch den Text weißt du sofort, dass es sich um ein Snowboard handeln müsste.

Es geht um *fraghwert*.

Ein *fraghwert* muss ein Sportgerät sein. Die Informationen über das *fraghwert* ergeben, dass es ein Snowboard ist.

In the supermarket you can buy vegetables, for example potatoes, tomatoes, carrots and cauliflowers. → Auch bei cauliflower muss es sich um ein Gemüse handeln (Blumenkohl).

Du kennst das Wort *friend*, das unbekannte Wort *friendship* könnte also *Freundschaft* bedeuten.
comfortable → komfortabel, bequem

122

7.4 Besser lesen und verstehen

ÜBUNG 13 Versuche die Bedeutung der folgenden Wörter herauszufinden, ohne ein Wörterbuch zu benutzen.

menswear

glow-worm

balcony

whelp

central heating

indoors

ÜBUNG 14 Du musst nicht jedes Wort verstehen, um den Inhalt eines Textes zu erfassen. Versuche bei der folgenden E-Mail herauszufinden, was das unterstrichene Wort bedeutet.

Dear Jack,
You have to get Jufawhety! It is so exciting. My brother put the CD-ROM in his computer and played Jufawhety all day. I had to wait three hours until I could test Jufawhety, too. It's about a castle. You have to find the way to the treasure chamber (Schatzkammer) with lots of gold and diamonds. Jufawhety is fantastic. If you want, you can borrow it sometime from me. Write back soon!
Yours, Tom

Jufawhety is:

WISSEN

Wortfelder und Wortfamilien
Ein **Wortfeld** umfasst Wörter, die dem Sinn oder der Bedeutung nach zusammengehören.

Wortfeld „sich fortbewegen": to go, to run, to jump, to jog, to ride
Wortfeld „Verkehrsmittel": car, bike, motorcycle, train, plane

In einer **Wortfamilie** sind Wörter gleicher Herkunft enthalten.

Wortfamilie „tanzen": to dance, dancer, dance hall, dance floor
Wortfamilie „schlafen": to sleep, sleeping bag, sleepy

Englisch lernen

 ÜBUNG 15 In dieser Wortschlange befinden sich zehn Gegenteilpaare. Finde sie heraus. Achte auf die Verben im Infinitiv (mit to)!

poorfatshorttostoptorememberrightyounghungrythirstyoldexpensivethinsmallboringtalloooheightottoforgetbigtointerestingtratstotpaehcirgnorw

big ↔ small

 ÜBUNG 16 Hier sind verschiedene Wortfamilien und Wortfelder durcheinandergeraten. Ordne die einzelnen Wörter den richtigen Boxen zu. Benenne das Wortfeld bzw. die Wortfamilie.

to shout – lemon – to say – life – to speak – to live – fruit juice – living room – banana – to talk – orange – fruitless – fruit salad – lively – fruity – kiwi

Klassenarbeit 1

Klassenarbeiten

60 Minuten

AUFGABE 1 Alphabettraining – Trage die passenden Buchstaben ein.

1. Trage den Buchstaben davor und danach ein!

   ▢ V ▢   ▢ I ▢   ▢ S ▢   ▢ B ▢   ▢ G ▢   ▢ M ▢

2. Wie heißt der übernächste Buchstabe?

   H ▢   E ▢   I ▢   O ▢   N ▢   W ▢   H ▢   R ▢

3. Wie heißt der vorletzte Buchstabe?

   ▢ K   ▢ E   ▢ L   ▢ O   ▢ D   ▢ N   ▢ S   ▢ W

AUFGABE 2 Im Folgenden stehen die beiden Leitwörter einer Seite im Wörterbuch. Markiere die Wörter, die dazwischenpassen.

murder – near: mystery – museum – neat – mum – mushroom – narrow
wear – white: who – why – weather – welcome – we – went – Welsh
million – mister: minor – miserable – mind – mile – minibus – mirror
early – else: emancipate – eighth – edge – earth – egg – ear – earl
lift – load: list – limit – loan – lock – light – lie – like – litter – lounge

AUFGABE 3 Verbessere die durcheinandergeratenen Sätze und trage sie hinter die passende Situation ein.

feeling / well / I / not / am
nice / have / weekend / a
help / can / me / you

word / spell / could / you / this / please
with / agree / you / I / do / not
you / write / it / please / on / board / the / could

Dir geht es nicht gut. → _____.

Du weißt nicht, wie man ein Wort schreibt. → _____
_____.

Freitags: Du verabschiedest dich. → _____.

Du bist nicht einverstanden. → _____.

Du brauchst Hilfe. → _____.

Du willst, dass dein Lehrer ein Wort an die Tafel schreibt. → _____
_____.

TESTEN

125

Englisch lernen

AUFGABE 4 Übersetze die folgenden Sätze.

Wie buchstabiert man dieses Wort?

Die Geschichte ist interessant / langweilig / lustig.

Du fängst an. Und dann bin ich an der Reihe.

AUFGABE 5 Englisch im Alltag – finde die richtige Frage oder gib eine passende Antwort.

1. The shop assistant in the bakery: "   "

   You: "No, that's all. How much is it?"

2. A tourist: "Can you tell me the way to the town hall *(Rathaus)*, please?"

   You: "   "

3. Your bike has a flat tyre *(Reifenpanne)*. You to a friend: "

   "

   Your friend: "Yes, of course. I will help you fix *(reparieren)* it."

4. Your mum: "What would you like for dinner?"

   You: "   "

5. Teacher: "   "

   You: "No, I haven't. I understood everything."

Das 3-fach-Prinzip für bessere Noten

Die Lernhilfenreihe „Wissen • Üben • Testen" mit den drei Bausteinen und echten Klassenarbeiten für gezielte Vorbereitung!

Jetzt neu:

- Rund 15 Testklassenarbeiten pro Band
- Separates Lösungsheft
- Englisch-Titel inklusive Audio-CD mit Übungen zum Hörverstehen

„Wissen • Üben • Testen" gibt es für die 5. bis 10. Klasse und die Fächer Deutsch, Mathematik und Englisch

www.lernhelfer.de

Stichwortfinder

A Adjektive 5
– regelmäßige Steigerung 5
– unregelmäßige
  Steigerung 7
– Stellung im Satz 8
– Vergleich 5
Adverbien 9
– Satzstellung 12
– Steigerung 9
– Vergleich 9
– verschiedene Arten 10
any 105
Aussagesätze
– bejahte 76
– verneinte 79

B Bedingungssätze 83
– Verneinung 84
Bindewörter 76

C *can / could* 21

F *for* 48
Frageanhängsel 100, 104
Fragen 99
– Entscheidungsfragen 99
– Ergänzungsfragen 99 f.
– Frageanhängsel *(question
  tags)* 100, 104
– im *past progressive* 99
– im *present perfect* 106
– im *simple past* 99
– Kurzantworten *(short
  answers)* 103

G *going to-future* 66
– Fragen 70
– Kurzformen 68

H Hilfsverben → modale
  Hilfsverben
Hörverstehen 116

I *if* 83

K Konjunktionen 76
Kurzantworten 103

L Lautschrift 114

M Mengenangaben 105
modale Hilfsverben 21
– dürfen *(to be allowed to,
  mustn't)* 23
– Fragen / Verneinungen 27
– können *(can, could,
  to be able to)* 21
– müssen *(must, to have
  (got) to)* 25
must 25
mustn't 23, 28

N *needn't* 28

P *past progressive* 41
– Signalwörter 42
present perfect 44 f.
– Fragen / Verneinungen 45
– Signalwörter 45

Q *question tags* 100, 104

R Relativsätze 86
– mit Relativpronomen 87
– nicht notwendige 86
– notwendige 86, 91
– ohne Relativpronomen 87

S *short answers* 103
simple past 34, 37 f.
– Fragen / Verneinungen 38
– regelmäßige Verben 34
– Signalwörter 34
– unregelmäßige Verben 37
since 48
some 105

T *to be able to* 21
to be allowed to 23
to have (got) to 25

U unregelmäßige Verben 52

V Vergangenheit 34
– *simple past* 34, 37 f.
– *past progressive* 41
– *present perfect* 44 f.

W *will-future* 63
– Fragen 70
– Kurzformen 64
– Signalwörter 65
when 83
Wörterbucharbeit 112 ff.
Wortfamilien und -felder 124

Z Zukunft 63
– *going to-future* 66
– *will-future* 63